Just The
facts101
Textbook Key Facts

Textbook Outlines, Highlights, and Practice Quizzes

Pharmacology for the Primary Care Provider

by Marilyn Winterton Edmunds, 4th Edition

All "Just the Facts101" Material Written or Prepared by Cram101 Textbook Reviews

Title Page

LEARNING SYSTEM

"Just the Facts101" is a Content Technologies publication and tool designed to give you all the facts from your textbooks. Register for the full practice test for each of your chapters for virtually any of your textbooks.

Facts101 has built custom study tools specific to your textbook. We provide all of the factual testable information and unlike traditional study guides, we will never send you back to your textbook for more information.

YOU WILL NEVER HAVE TO HIGHLIGHT A BOOK AGAIN!

Facts101 StudyGuides

All of the information in this StudyGuide is written specifically for your textbook. We include the key terms, places, people, and concepts... the information you can expect on your next exam!

Facts101

Only Facts101 gives you the outlines, highlights, and PRACTICE TESTS specific to your textbook. Facts101 sister Cram101.com is an online application where you'll discover study tools designed to make the most of your limited study time.

www.Cram101.com

STUDYING MADE EASY

This Cram101 notebook is designed to make studying easier and increase your comprehension of the textbook material. Instead of starting with a blank notebook and trying to write down everything discussed in class lectures, you can use this Cram101 textbook notebook and annotate your notes along with the lecture.

Our goal is to give you the best tools for success.

For a supreme understanding of the course, pair your notebook with our online tools at www.cram101.com

Our Online Access program is a simple way for us to keep our promise and provide you the best studying tools, regardless of where you purchased your Cram101 textbook notebook. As long as you let us know you are intereested in a free online access account we will set it up for you for 180 days.

Online Access:

SIMPLE STEPS TO GET A FREE ACCOUNT:
Email Travis.Reese@cram101.com
Include:
Order number
ISBN of Guide
Retailer where purchased

Pharmacology for the Primary Care Provider
Marilyn Winterton Edmunds, 4th

CONTENTS

CHAPTER OUTLINE: KEY TERMS, PEOPLE, PLACES, CONCEPTS

	Duloxetine
	Antihypertensive
	Loratadine
	Serotonin
	Pharmaceutical industry
	Phosphodiesterase
	Doctor of Pharmacy
	Menstrual cycle
	Esmolol
	Polymyxin
	Monoamine oxidase inhibitors

CHAPTER HIGHLIGHTS & NOTES: KEY TERMS, PEOPLE, PLACES, CONCEPTS

Duloxetine	Duloxetine (sold under the brand names Cymbalta, Ariclaim, Xeristar, Yentreve, Duzela) is a serotonin-norepinephrine reuptake inhibitor (SNRI) manufactured and marketed by Eli Lilly. It is effective for major depressive disorder and generalized anxiety disorder (GAD). Duloxetine failed the US approval for stress urinary incontinence amidst concerns over liver toxicity and suicidal events; however, it was approved for this indication in Europe, where it is recommended as an add-on medication in stress urinary incontinence instead of surgery.
Antihypertensive	Antihypertensives are a class of drugs that are used to treat hypertension (high blood pressure). Antihypertensive therapy seeks to prevent the complications of high blood pressure, such as stroke and myocardial infarction. Evidence suggests that reduction of the blood pressure by 5 mmHg can decrease the risk of stroke by 34%, of ischaemic heart disease by 21%, and reduce the likelihood of dementia, heart failure, and mortality from cardiovascular disease.

1. UNIT-1 Foundations of Prescriptive Practice,

Loratadine	Loratadine (INN) is a second-generation H_1 histamine antagonist drug used to treat allergies. Structurally, it is closely related to tricyclic antidepressants, such as imipramine, and is distantly related to the atypical antipsychotic quetiapine.
	Loratadine is marketed by Schering-Plough under several trade names (e.g., Claritin) and also by Shionogi in Japan. It is available as a generic drug and is marketed for its non-sedating properties. In a version named Claritin-D or Clarinase, it is combined with pseudoephedrine, a decongestant; this makes it useful for colds as well as allergies but adds potential side-effects of insomnia, anxiety, and nervousness.
Serotonin	Serotonin or 5-hydroxytryptamine (5-HT) is a monoamine neurotransmitter. Biochemically derived from tryptophan, serotonin is primarily found in the gastrointestinal (GI) tract, platelets, and in the central nervous system (CNS) of animals including humans. It is popularly thought to be a contributor to feelings of well-being and happiness.
Pharmaceutical industry	The pharmaceutical industry develops, produces, and markets drugs or pharmaceuticals licensed for use as medications. Pharmaceutical companies are allowed to deal in generic and/or brand medications and medical devices. They are subject to a variety of laws and regulations regarding the patenting, testing and ensuring safety and efficacy and marketing of drugs.
Phosphodiesterase	A phosphodiesterase is any enzyme that breaks a phosphodiester bond. Usually, people speaking of phosphodiesterase are referring to cyclic nucleotide phosphodiesterases, which have great clinical significance and are described below. However, there are many other families of phosphodiesterases, including phospholipases C and D, autotaxin, sphingomyelin phosphodiesterase, DNases, RNases, and restriction endonucleases (which all break the phosphodiester backbone of DNA or RNA), as well as numerous less-well-characterized small-molecule phosphodiesterases.
Doctor of Pharmacy	A Doctor of Pharmacy is a professional doctor degree in pharmacy. In some countries, it is a first professional degree, and a prerequisite for licensing to exercise the profession of Pharmacist.
Menstrual cycle	The menstrual cycle is the scientific term for the physiological changes that occur in fertile women and other female primates for the purposes of sexual reproduction.
	The menstrual cycle, under the control of the endocrine system, is necessary for reproduction. It is commonly divided into three phases: the follicular phase, ovulation, and the luteal phase.
Esmolol	Esmolol (trade name Brevibloc) is a cardioselective $beta_1$ receptor blocker with rapid onset, a very short duration of action, and no significant intrinsic sympathomimetic or membrane stabilising activity at therapeutic dosages.
	It is a class II antiarrhythmic.

	Esmolol decreases the force and rate of heart contractions by blocking beta-adrenergic receptors of the sympathetic nervous system, which are found in the heart and other organs of the body. Esmolol prevents the action of two naturally occurring substances: epinephrine and norepinephrine.
Polymyxin	Polymyxins are antibiotics, with a general structure consisting of a cyclic peptide with a long hydrophobic tail. They disrupt the structure of the bacterial cell membrane by interacting with its phospholipids. They are produced by nonribosomal peptide synthetase systems in Gram-positive bacteria such as Paenibacillus polymyxa and are selectively toxic for Gram-negative bacteria due to their specificity for the lipopolysaccharide molecule that exists within many Gram-negative outer membranes.
Monoamine oxidase inhibitors	Monoamine oxidase inhibitors (MAOIs) are chemicals which inhibit the activity of the monoamine oxidase enzyme family. They have a long history of use as medications prescribed for the treatment of depression. They are particularly effective in treating atypical depression. Because of potentially lethal dietary and drug interactions, monoamine oxidase inhibitors have historically been reserved as a last line of treatment, used only when other classes of antidepressant drugs (for example selective serotonin reuptake inhibitors and tricyclic antidepressants) have failed. A transdermal patch form of the MAOI selegiline, called Emsam, was approved for use by the Food and Drug Administration in the United States on February 28, 2006.

1. _____ or 5-hydroxytryptamine (5-HT) is a monoamine neurotransmitter. Biochemically derived from tryptophan, _____ is primarily found in the gastrointestinal (GI) tract, platelets, and in the central nervous system (CNS) of animals including humans. It is popularly thought to be a contributor to feelings of well-being and happiness.

   a. histamine
   b. monoamine
   c. 5-Hydroxytryptamine
   d. Serotonin

2. . The _____ is the scientific term for the physiological changes that occur in fertile women and other female primates for the purposes of sexual reproduction.

   The _____, under the control of the endocrine system, is necessary for reproduction. It is commonly divided into three phases: the follicular phase, ovulation, and the luteal phase.

    a. Menstrual cycle

    b. Homeopathic

    c. Chiropractic

    d. Hirudiculture

3. _____ (INN) is a second-generation H_1 histamine antagonist drug used to treat allergies. Structurally, it is closely related to tricyclic antidepressants, such as imipramine, and is distantly related to the atypical antipsychotic quetiapine.

_____ is marketed by Schering-Plough under several trade names (e.g., Claritin) and also by Shionogi in Japan. It is available as a generic drug and is marketed for its non-sedating properties. In a version named Claritin-D or Clarinase, it is combined with pseudoephedrine, a decongestant; this makes it useful for colds as well as allergies but adds potential side-effects of insomnia, anxiety, and nervousness.

    a. Loratadine

    b. Loratadine

    c. Chiropractic

    d. Pepto-Bismol

4. _____ (MAOIs) are chemicals which inhibit the activity of the monoamine oxidase enzyme family. They have a long history of use as medications prescribed for the treatment of depression. They are particularly effective in treating atypical depression.

Because of potentially lethal dietary and drug interactions, _____ have historically been reserved as a last line of treatment, used only when other classes of antidepressant drugs (for example selective serotonin reuptake inhibitors and tricyclic antidepressants) have failed. A transdermal patch form of the MAOI selegiline, called Emsam, was approved for use by the Food and Drug Administration in the United States on February 28, 2006.

    a. Monoamine oxidase inhibitors

    b. isomer

    c. Chiropractic

    d. Hirudiculture

5. . A _____ is any enzyme that breaks a phosphodiester bond. Usually, people speaking of _____ are referring to cyclic nucleotide _____s, which have great clinical significance and are described below. However, there are many other families of _____s, including phospholipases C and D, autotaxin, sphingomyelin _____, DNases, RNases, and restriction endonucleases (which all break the phosphodiester backbone of DNA or RNA), as well as numerous less-well-characterized small-molecule _____s.

    a. Phosphodiesterase

    b. Pharmaconomy

    c. Pharmacovigilance

ANSWER KEY
1. UNIT-1 Foundations of Prescriptive Practice,

1. d
2. a
3. b
4. a
5. a

You can take the complete Online Interactive Chapter Practice Test

for 1. UNIT-1 Foundations of Prescriptive Practice,
on all key terms, persons, places, and concepts.

No Additional Costs

http://www.Cram101.com

Register, send an email request to Travis.Reese@Cram101.com to get your user Id and password.

Include your customer order number, and ISBN number from your studyguide Retailer.

2. UNIT-2 Pharmacokinetics and Pharmacodynamics,

CHAPTER OUTLINE: KEY TERMS, PEOPLE, PLACES, CONCEPTS

	Pharmacodynamics
	Pharmacokinetics
	Nomenclature
	Buccal administration
	Oral administration
	Sublingual administration
	Active transport
	Biotransformation
	Drug metabolism
	Creatinine clearance
	Potency
	Side effect
	Cyclosporine
	Monoamine oxidase inhibitors
	Quinolones
	Mechanism of action
	Chamomile
	Dong quai
	Garlic
	Atropine
	Circadian rhythm

Toxicity

Therapeutic index

Therapeutic window

Maintenance dose

Loading dose

Geriatric

Obsessive-compulsive disorder

Serotonin syndrome

Beers List

Menstrual cycle

Gray baby syndrome

Plasma protein binding

Renal failure

Amikacin

Body surface area

Clark's rule

Minocycline

Nitrofurantoin

Potassium chloride

Probenecid

Cefaclor

2. UNIT-2 Pharmacokinetics and Pharmacodynamics,

CHAPTER OUTLINE: KEY TERMS, PEOPLE, PLACES, CONCEPTS

	Cocaine
	Primidone
	Dimenhydrinate
	Diphenhydramine
	Ethambutol
	Metoclopramide
	Ondansetron
	Promethazine
	Pyridoxine
	Vancomycin
	Citalopram
	Fluoxetine
	Phenelzine
	Rubella vaccine
	Nicotine
	Azithromycin
	Ceftriaxone
	Cetirizine
	Cromoglicic acid
	Famciclovir
	Glipizide

	Glibenclamide
	Hydrochlorothiazide
	Insulin
	Metoprolol tartrate
	Miconazole
	Ofloxacin
	Omeprazole
	Paroxetine
	Permethrin
	Prednisolone
	Propranolol
	Ranitidine
	Salmeterol
	Tobramycin
	Tretinoin
	Valacyclovir
	Zafirlukast
	Lactation
	Sodium
	Alternative medicine
	Integrative medicine

2. UNIT-2 Pharmacokinetics and Pharmacodynamics,

CHAPTER OUTLINE: KEY TERMS, PEOPLE, PLACES, CONCEPTS

Traditional Chinese medicine

Echinacea

Melatonin

Kava

Herbal medicine

Standardization

Feverfew

Green tea

Comfrey

Germander

Lobelia

Mandrake

Yohimbe

2. UNIT-2 Pharmacokinetics and Pharmacodynamics,

Pharmacodynamics	Pharmacodynamics is the study of the biochemical and physiological effects of drugs on the body or on microorganisms or parasites within or on the body and the mechanisms of drug action and the relationship between drug concentration and effect. One dominant example is drug-receptor interactions as modeled by $L + R \rightleftharpoons L \cdot R$ where L=ligand (drug), R=receptor (attachment site), reaction dynamics that can be studied mathematically through tools such as free energy maps. Pharmacodynamics is often summarized as the study of what a drug does to the body, whereas pharmacokinetics is the study of what the body does to a drug.
Pharmacokinetics	Pharmacokinetics, is a branch of pharmacology dedicated to the determination of the fate of substances administered externally to a living organism. The substances of interest include pharmaceutical agents, hormones, nutrients, and toxins. Pharmacokinetics includes the study of the mechanisms of absorption and distribution of an administered drug, the chemical changes of the substance in the body (e.g. by metabolic enzymes such as CYP or UGT enzymes), and the effects and routes of excretion of the metabolites of the drug.
Nomenclature	Nomenclature is a term that applies to either a list of names or terms, or to refer to something that is a term or to the system of principles, procedures and terms related to naming-which is the assigning of a word or phrase to a particular object, event, or property. The principles of naming vary from the relatively informal conventions of everyday speech to the internationally-agreed principles, rules and recommendations that govern the formation and use of the specialist terms used in scientific and other disciplines. Naming 'things' is a part of our general communication using words and language: it is an aspect of everyday taxonomy as we distinguish the objects of our experience, together with their similarities and differences, which we identify, name and classify.
Buccal administration	Buccal administration refers to the pharmacological route of administration by which drugs diffuse into the blood through tissues of the buccal vestibule, the area inside the mouth between the lining of cheek (the buccal mucosa) and the teeth / gums. Certain medications are designed to be given bucally (as opposed to orally or sublingually). Buccal (as opposed to oral) administration usually results in a more rapid onset of action, since the medication need not pass through the digestive system and can be absorbed directly through the skin.
Oral administration	Oral administration is a route of administration where a substance is taken through the mouth. Many medications are taken orally because they are intended to have a systemic effect, reaching different parts of the body via the bloodstream, for example.

Sublingual administration	Sublingual, literally 'under the tongue', from Latin, refers to the pharmacological route of administration by which drugs diffuse into the blood through tissues under the tongue. Many pharmaceuticals are designed for sublingual administration, including cardiovascular drugs, steroids, barbiturates, enzymes, and increasingly, vitamins and minerals.
Active transport	Active transport is the movement of molecules across a cell membrane in the direction against their concentration gradient, i.e. moving from a low concentration to a high concentration. Active transport is usually associated with accumulating high concentrations of molecules that the cell needs, such as ions, glucose and amino acids. If the process uses chemical energy, such as from adenosine triphosphate (ATP), it is termed primary active transport.
Biotransformation	Biotransformation is the chemical modification made by an organism on a chemical compound. If this modification ends in mineral compounds like CO_2, NH_4^+, or H_2O, the biotransformation is called mineralisation. Biotransformation means chemical alteration of chemicals such as (but not limited to) nutrients, amino acids, toxins, and drugs in the body.
Drug metabolism	Drug metabolism also known as xenobiotic metabolism is the biochemical modification of pharmaceutical substances or xenobiotics respectively by living organisms, usually through specialized enzymatic systems. Drug metabolism often converts lipophilic chemical compounds into more readily excreted hydrophilic products. The rate of metabolism determines the duration and intensity of a drug's pharmacological action.
Creatinine clearance	Renal function, in nephrology, is an indication of the state of the kidney and its role in renal physiology. Glomerular filtration rate (GFR) describes the flow rate of filtered fluid through the kidney. Creatinine clearance rate (C_{Cr} or CrCl) is the volume of blood plasma that is cleared of creatinine per unit time and is a useful measure for approximating the GFR. Creatinine clearance exceeds GFR due to creatinine secretion, which can be blocked by cimetidine.
Potency	In the field of pharmacology, potency is a measure of drug activity expressed in terms of the amount required to produce an effect of given intensity. A highly potent drug (e.g., morphine, alprazolam, chlorpromazine) evokes a larger response at low concentrations, while a drug of lower potency evokes a small response at low concentrations. It is proportional to affinity and efficacy.
Side effect	In medicine, a side effect is an effect, whether therapeutic or adverse, that is secondary to the one intended; although the term is predominantly employed to describe adverse effects, it can also apply to beneficial, but unintended, consequences of the use of a drug. Occasionally, drugs are prescribed or procedures performed specifically for their side effects; in that case, said side effect ceases to be a side effect, and is now an intended effect.

2. UNIT-2 Pharmacokinetics and Pharmacodynamics,

Cyclosporine	Ciclosporin (INNBAN), cyclosporine cyclosporin (former BAN), or cyclosporin A (often shortened to CsA) is an immunosuppressant drug widely used in organ transplantation to prevent rejection. It reduces the activity of the immune system by interfering with the activity and growth of T cells. It was initially isolated from the fungus Tolypocladium inflatum (Beauveria nivea), found in a soil sample obtained in 1969 from Hardangervidda, Norway by Dr. Hans Peter Frey, a Sandoz biologist.
Monoamine oxidase inhibitors	Monoamine oxidase inhibitors (MAOIs) are chemicals which inhibit the activity of the monoamine oxidase enzyme family. They have a long history of use as medications prescribed for the treatment of depression. They are particularly effective in treating atypical depression. Because of potentially lethal dietary and drug interactions, monoamine oxidase inhibitors have historically been reserved as a last line of treatment, used only when other classes of antidepressant drugs (for example selective serotonin reuptake inhibitors and tricyclic antidepressants) have failed. A transdermal patch form of the MAOI selegiline, called Emsam, was approved for use by the Food and Drug Administration in the United States on February 28, 2006.
Quinolones	The quinolones are a family of synthetic broad-spectrum antibacterial drugs The first generation of the quinolones began with the introduction of nalidixic acid in 1962 for treatment of urinary tract infections in humans. Nalidixic acid was discovered by George Lesher and coworkers in a distillate during an attempt at chloroquine synthesis. They prevent bacterial DNA from unwinding and duplicating.
Mechanism of action	In pharmacology, the term mechanism of action refers to the specific biochemical interaction through which a drug substance produces its pharmacological effect. A mechanism of action usually includes mention of the specific molecular targets to which the drug binds, such as an enzyme or receptor. For example, the mechanism of action of aspirin involves irreversible inhibition of the enzyme cyclooxygenase, therefore suppressing the production of prostaglandins and thromboxanes, thereby reducing pain and inflammation.
Chamomile	Chamomile is a common name for several daisy-like plants of the family Asteraceae. These plants are best known for their ability to be made into an infusion which is commonly used to help with sleep and is often served with honey or lemon, or both. Chemical compounds present within chamomile have demonstrated the ability to bind GABA receptors, modulate monoamine neurotransmission, and have displayed neuroendocrine effects. Major chemical compounds present within chamomile include apigenin and alpha-bisabolol. There is Level B evidence to support the claim that chamomile possesses anxiolytic (anti-anxiety) properties and chamomile may have clinical applications in the treatment of stress and insomnia.

CHAPTER HIGHLIGHTS & NOTES: KEY TERMS, PEOPLE, PLACES, CONCEPTS

Dong quai	Angelica sinensis, commonly known as dong quai or 'female ginseng' is a herb from the family Apiaceae, indigenous to China.
Garlic	Allium sativum, commonly known as garlic, is a species in the onion genus, Allium. Its close relatives include the onion, shallot, leek, chive, and rakkyo. Dating back over 6,000 years, garlic is native to central Asia, and has long been a staple in the Mediterranean region, as well as a frequent seasoning in Asia, Africa, and Europe.
Atropine	Atropine is a naturally occurring tropane alkaloid extracted from deadly nightshade (Atropa belladonna), Jimson weed (Datura stramonium), mandrake (Mandragora officinarum) and other plants of the family Solanaceae. It is a secondary metabolite of these plants and serves as a drug with a wide variety of effects. In general, atropine counters the 'rest and digest' activity of all muscles and glands regulated by the parasympathetic nervous system.
Circadian rhythm	A circadian rhythm is any biological process that displays an endogenous, entrainable oscillation of about 24 hours. These 24-hour rhythms are driven by a circadian clock, and they have been widely observed in plants, animals, fungi, and cyanobacteria. The term circadian comes from the Latin circa, meaning 'around' (or 'approximately'), and diem or dies, meaning 'day'.
Toxicity	Toxicity is the degree to which a substance can damage an organism. Toxicity can refer to the effect on a whole organism, such as an animal, bacterium, or plant, as well as the effect on a substructure of the organism, such as a cell (cytotoxicity) or an organ such as the liver (hepatotoxicity). By extension, the word may be metaphorically used to describe toxic effects on larger and more complex groups, such as the family unit or society at large.
Therapeutic index	The therapeutic index is a comparison of the amount of a therapeutic agent that causes the therapeutic effect to the amount that causes death (in animal studies) or toxicity (in human studies). Quantitatively, it is the ratio given by the lethal or toxic dose divided by the therapeutic dose. In animal studies, the therapeutic index is the lethal dose of a drug for 50% of the population (LD_{50}) divided by the minimum effective dose for 50% of the population (ED_{50}).
Therapeutic window	The Therapeutic window of a drug is the range of drug dosages which can treat disease effectively while staying within the safety range. In other words, it is the dosages of a medication between the amount that gives an effect (effective dose) and the amount that gives more adverse effects than desired effects. For instance, medication with a small pharmaceutical window such as Tegretol must be administered with care and control, e.g. by frequently measuring blood concentration of the drug, since it easily gives adverse effects such as agranulocytosis.
Maintenance dose	A maintenance dose is the maintenance rate [mg/h] of drug administration equal to the rate of elimination at steady state.

This is not to be confused with a dose regimen, which is a type of drug therapy in which the dose [mg] of a drug is given at a regular dosing interval on a repetitive basis. Continuing the maintenance dose for about 4 to 5 half lives ($t_{½}$) of the drug will approximate the steady state level.

Loading dose	A loading dose is an initial higher dose of a drug that may be given at the beginning of a course of treatment before dropping down to a lower maintenance dose. A loading dose is most useful for drugs that are eliminated from the body relatively slowly. Such drugs need only a low maintenance dose in order to keep the amount of the drug in the body at the appropriate level, but this also means that, without an initial higher dose, it would take a long time for the amount of the drug in the body to reach that level.
Geriatric	Geriatrics or geriatric medicine is a specialty that focuses on health care of elderly people. It aims to promote health by preventing and treating diseases and disabilities in older adults. There is no set age at which patients may be under the care of a geriatrician or geriatric physician, a physician who specializes in the care of elderly people.
Obsessive-compulsive disorder	Obsessive-compulsive disorder is an anxiety disorder characterized by intrusive thoughts that produce uneasiness, apprehension, fear, or worry; by repetitive behaviors aimed at reducing the associated anxiety; or by a combination of such obsessions and compulsions. Symptoms of the disorder include excessive washing or cleaning; repeated checking; extreme hoarding; preoccupation with sexual, violent or religious thoughts; relationship-related obsessions; aversion to particular numbers; and nervous rituals, such as opening and closing a door a certain number of times before entering or leaving a room. These symptoms can be alienating and time-consuming, and often cause severe emotional and financial distress.
Serotonin syndrome	Serotonin syndrome is a potentially life-threatening adverse drug reaction that may occur following therapeutic drug use, inadvertent interactions between drugs, overdose of particular drugs, or the recreational use of certain drugs. Serotonin syndrome is not an idiosyncratic drug reaction; it is a predictable consequence of excess serotonergic activity at central nervous system (CNS) and peripheral serotonin receptors. For this reason, some experts strongly prefer the terms serotonin toxicity or serotonin toxidrome because these more accurately reflect the fact that it is a form of poisoning.
Beers List	The Beers Criteria for Potentially Inappropriate Medication Use in Older Adults, commonly called the Beers List, is a guideline for healthcare professionals to help improve the safety of prescribing medications for older adults. It emphasizes deprescribing medication that is unnecessary health care, which reduces the problems of high risk-benefit ratio, polypharmacy, drug interactions, and adverse drug reactions. The criteria are used in geriatrics clinical care to monitor and improve the quality of healthcare.

CHAPTER HIGHLIGHTS & NOTES: KEY TERMS, PEOPLE, PLACES, CONCEPTS

Menstrual cycle	The menstrual cycle is the scientific term for the physiological changes that occur in fertile women and other female primates for the purposes of sexual reproduction. The menstrual cycle, under the control of the endocrine system, is necessary for reproduction. It is commonly divided into three phases: the follicular phase, ovulation, and the luteal phase.
Gray baby syndrome	Gray baby syndrome is a rare but serious side effect that occurs in newborn infants (especially premature babies) following the intravenous administration of the antimicrobial chloramphenicol.
Plasma protein binding	A drug's efficiency may be affected by the degree to which it binds to the proteins within blood plasma. The less bound a drug is, the more efficiently it can traverse cell membranes or diffuse. Common blood proteins that drugs bind to are human serum albumin, lipoprotein, glycoprotein, α, β, and γ globulins. A drug in blood exists in two forms: bound and unbound. Depending on a specific drug's affinity for plasma protein, a proportion of the drug may become bound to plasma proteins, with the remainder being unbound. If the protein binding is reversible, then a chemical equilibrium will exist between the bound and unbound states, such that:Protein + drug ⇌ Protein-drug complex Notably, it is the unbound fraction which exhibits pharmacologic effects. It is also the fraction that may be metabolized and/or excreted. For example, the 'fraction bound' of the anticoagulant warfarin is 97%. This means that of the amount of warfarin in the blood, 97% is bound to plasma proteins. The remaining 3% (the fraction unbound) is the fraction that is actually active and may be excreted. Protein binding can influence the drug's biological half-life in the body. The bound portion may act as a reservoir or depot from which the drug is slowly released as the unbound form. Since the unbound form is being metabolized and/or excreted from the body, the bound fraction will be released in order to maintain equilibrium. Since albumin is basic, acidic and neutral drugs will primarily bind to albumin. If albumin becomes saturated, then these drugs will bind to lipoprotein. Basic drugs will bind to the acidic alpha-1 acid glycoprotein. This is significant because various medical conditions may affect the levels of albumin, alpha-1 acid glycoprotein, and lipoproteins. Impact of the altered protein binding Only the unbound fraction of the drug undergoes metabolism in the liver and other tissues. As the drug dissociates from the protein more and more drug undergoes metabolism. Changes in the levels of free drug change the volume of distribution because free drug may distribute into the tissues leading to a decrease in plasma concentration profile. For the drugs which rapidly undergo metabolism, clearance is dependent on the hepatic blood flow. For drugs which slowly undergo metabolism, changes in the unbound fraction of the drug directly change the clearance of the drug.

Note: The most commonly used methods for measuring drug concentration levels in the plasma measure bound as well as unbound fractions of the drug.

The fraction unbound can be altered by a number of variables, such as the concentration of drug in the body, the amount and quality of plasma protein, and other drugs that bind to plasma proteins. Higher drug concentrations would lead to a higher fraction unbound, because the plasma protein would be saturated with drug and any excess drug would be unbound. If the amount of plasma protein is decreased (such as in catabolism, malnutrition, liver disease, renal disease), there would also be a higher fraction unbound. Additionally, the quality of the plasma protein may affect how many drug-binding sites there are on the protein. Drug interactions

Using 2 drugs at the same time may affect each other's fraction unbound. For example, assume that Drug A and Drug B are both protein-bound drugs. If Drug A is given, it will bind to the plasma proteins in the blood. If Drug B is also given, it can displace Drug A from the protein, thereby increasing Drug A's fraction unbound. This may increase the effects of Drug A, since only the unbound fraction may exhibit activity. This change in pharmacologic effect could have adverse consequences.

This effect of protein binding is most significant with drugs that are highly protein-bound (>95%) and have a low therapeutic index, such as warfarin. A low therapeutic index indicates that there is a high risk of toxicity when using the drug. Since warfarin is an anticoagulant with a low therapeutic index, warfarin may cause bleeding if the correct degree of pharmacologic effect is not maintained. If a patient on warfarin takes another drug that displaces warfarin from plasma protein, such as a sulfonamide antibiotic, it could result in an increased risk of bleeding. Plasma protein binding prediction software •Quantum Plasma Protein Binding•S+ Plasma Protein Binding•Albumin binding prediction.

Renal failure	Renal failure is a medical condition in which the kidneys fail to adequately filter waste products from the blood. The two main forms are acute kidney injury, which is often reversible with adequate treatment, and chronic kidney disease, which is often not reversible. In both cases, there is usually an underlying cause.
Amikacin	Amikacin is an aminoglycoside antibiotic used to treat different types of bacterial infections. Amikacin works by binding to the bacterial 30S ribosomal subunit, causing misreading of mRNA and leaving the bacterium unable to synthesize proteins vital to its growth.
Body surface area	In physiology and medicine, the body surface area is the measured or calculated surface area of a human body. For many clinical purposes Body surface area is a better indicator of metabolic mass than body weight because it is less affected by abnormal adipose mass. Nevertheless, there have been several important critiques of the use of Body surface area in determining the dosage of medications with a narrow therapeutic index like many chemotherapy medications.

Clark's rule	Clark's Rule is a medical term referring to a mathematical formula used to calculate the proper dosage of medicine for children aged 2-17. The procedure is to take the child's weight in pounds, divide by 150 lb, and multiply the fractional result by the adult dose to find the equivalent child dosage. For example: If an adult dose of medication calls for 30 mg and the child weighs 30 lb. Divide the weight by 150 (30/150) to get 1/5. Multiply 1/5 times 30 mg to get 6 mg.
Minocycline	Minocycline is a broad-spectrum tetracycline antibiotic, and has a broader spectrum than the other members of the group. It is a bacteriostatic antibiotic, classified as a long-acting type. As a result of its long half-life it generally has serum levels 2-4 times that of the simple water-soluble tetracyclines (150 mg giving 16 times the activity levels compared with 250 mg of tetracycline at 24-48 hours).
Nitrofurantoin	Nitrofurantoin is an antibiotic which is marketed under the following brand names; Niftran, Furadantin, Furabid, Macrobid, Macrodantin, Nitrofur Mac, Nitro Macro, Nifty-SR, Martifur-MR, Martifur-100 (in India), Urantoin, and Uvamin (in Middle East). It is usually used in treating urinary tract infection. Like many other drugs, it is often used against E. coli.
Potassium chloride	The chemical compound potassium chloride is a metal halide salt composed of potassium and chlorine. In its pure state, it is odorless and has a white or colorless vitreous crystal appearance, with a crystal structure that cleaves easily in three directions. Potassium chloride crystals are face-centered cubic.
Probenecid	Probenecid is a uricosuric drug that increases uric acid excretion in the urine. It is primarily used in treating gout and hyperuricemia. Probenecid was developed as an alternative to caronamide to competitively inhibit renal excretion of some drugs, thereby increasing their plasma concentration and prolonging their effects.
Cefaclor	Cefaclor, also known as cefachlor or cefaclorum, is a second-generation cephalosporin antibiotic used to treat certain infections caused by bacteria such as pneumonia and ear, lung, skin, throat, and urinary tract infections.
Cocaine	Cocaine (INN) is a crystalline tropane alkaloid that is obtained from the leaves of the coca plant. The name comes from 'coca' in addition to the alkaloid suffix -ine, forming cocaine. It is a stimulant of the central nervous system, an appetite suppressant, and a topical anesthetic.
Primidone	Primidone is an anticonvulsant of the pyrimidinedione class, the active metabolites of which, phenobarbital (major) and phenylethylmalonamide (PEMA) (minor), are also anticonvulsants. It is used mainly to treat complex partial, simple partial, generalized tonic-clonic seizures, myoclonic, and akinetic seizures. Since the 1980s it has been a valuable alternative to propranolol in the treatment of essential tremor.

2. UNIT-2 Pharmacokinetics and Pharmacodynamics,

Dimenhydrinate	Dimenhydrinate is an over-the-counter drug used to prevent nausea and motion sickness. It is marketed in Brazil as Dramin, in Canada as Gravol, in Ecuador as Anautin, in Hungary as Daedalon, in Italy as Xamamina, in Indonesia as Antimo, in Portugal as Viabom. It is most commonly used as pills, although it is also available in liquid form and in suppositories.
Diphenhydramine	Diphenhydramine is a first-generation antihistamine possessing anticholinergic, antitussive, antiemetic, and sedative properties that is mainly used to treat allergies. It is also used in the management of drug-induced parkinsonism and other extrapyramidal symptoms. The drug has a strong hypnotic effect and is FDA-approved as a non-prescription sleep aid, especially in the form of diphenhydramine citrate.
Ethambutol	Ethambutol is a bacteriostatic antimycobacterial drug prescribed to treat tuberculosis. It is usually given in combination with other tuberculosis drugs, such as isoniazid, rifampicin and pyrazinamide. It is sold under the trade names Myambutol and Servambutol.
Metoclopramide	Metoclopramide is an antiemetic and gastroprokinetic agent. It belongs to a group of medicines called ´dopaminergic´ blockers. It is commonly used to treat nausea and vomiting, to facilitate gastric emptying in people with gastroparesis, and as a treatment for the gastric stasis often associated with migraine headaches.
Ondansetron	Ondansetron is a serotonin 5-HT$_3$ receptor antagonist used mainly as an antiemetic (to treat nausea and vomiting), often following chemotherapy. It affects both peripheral and central nerves. Ondansetron reduces the activity of the vagus nerve, which deactivates the vomiting center in the medulla oblongata, and also blocks serotonin receptors in the chemoreceptor trigger zone.
Promethazine	Promethazine is a first-generation antihistamine of the phenothiazine family. The drug has anti-motion sickness, antiemetic, and anticholinergic effects, as well as a strong sedative effect and in some countries is prescribed for insomnia when benzodiazepines are contraindicated. It is available over-the-counter in the United Kingdom, Australia, Switzerland, and many other countries, but by prescription in the United States (brand names Phenergan, Promethegan, Romergan, Fargan, Farganesse, Prothiazine, Avomine, Atosil, Receptozine, Lergigan, and Sominex in the UK).
Pyridoxine	Pyridoxine is one of the compounds that can be called vitamin B$_6$, along with pyridoxal and pyridoxamine. It differs from pyridoxamine by the substituent at the '4' position. Its hydrochloride salt pyridoxine hydrochloride is often used.
Vancomycin	Vancomycin INN is a glycopeptide antibiotic used in the prophylaxis and treatment of infections caused by Gram-positive bacteria. Vancomycin was first isolated in 1953 at Eli Lilly, from a soil sample collected from the interior jungles of Borneo by a missionary.

CHAPTER HIGHLIGHTS & NOTES: KEY TERMS, PEOPLE, PLACES, CONCEPTS

Citalopram	Citalopram is an antidepressant drug of the selective serotonin reuptake inhibitor (SSRI) class. It has U.S. Food and Drug Administration (FDA) approval to treat major depression, and is prescribed off-label for other conditions. In UK, Germany, Portugal, Poland, and most European countries it is licenced for depressive episodes and panic disorder with or without agoraphobia.
Fluoxetine	Fluoxetine (also known by the tradenames Prozac, Sarafem, Fontex, among others) is an antidepressant of the selective serotonin reuptake inhibitor (SSRI) class. Fluoxetine was first documented in 1974 by scientists from Eli Lilly and Company. It was presented to the U.S. Food and Drug Administration in February 1977, with Eli Lilly receiving final approval to market the drug in December 1987. Fluoxetine went off-patent in August 2001.
Phenelzine	Phenelzine is a non-selective and irreversible monoamine oxidase inhibitor (MAOI) of the hydrazine class which is used as an antidepressant and anxiolytic. Along with tranylcypromine and isocarboxazid, phenelzine is one of the few non-selective MAOIs still in widespread clinical use. It is typically available in 15 mg tablets and doses usually range from 30-90 mg per day, with 15 mg every day or every other day suggested as a maintenance dose following a successful course of treatment.
Rubella vaccine	Rubella vaccine is a vaccine used against rubella. One form is called 'Meruvax'.
Nicotine	Nicotine is an alkaloid found in the nightshade family of plants (Solanaceae) that constitutes approximately 0.6-3.0% of the dry weight of tobacco, with biosynthesis taking place in the roots and accumulation occurring in the leaves. It functions as an antiherbivore chemical with particular specificity to insects; therefore nicotine was widely used as an insecticide in the past, and currently nicotine analogs such as imidacloprid continue to be widely used. In low concentrations (an average cigarette yields about 1 mg of absorbed nicotine), the substance acts as a stimulant in mammals and is the main factor responsible for the dependence-forming properties of tobacco smoking.
Azithromycin	Azithromycin is an azalide, a subclass of macrolide antibiotics. Azithromycin is one of the world's best-selling antibiotics. It is derived from erythromycin, with a methyl-substituted nitrogen atom incorporated into the lactone ring, thus making the lactone ring 15-membered.
Ceftriaxone	Ceftriaxone is a third-generation cephalosporin antibiotic. Like other third-generation cephalosporins, it has broad spectrum activity against Gram-positive and Gram-negative bacteria. In most cases, it is considered to be equivalent to cefotaxime in terms of safety and efficacy.
Cetirizine	Cetirizine, a second-generation antihistamine used in the treatment of allergies, hay fever, angioedema, and urticaria. It is a major metabolite of hydroxyzine, and a racemic selective H_1 receptor inverse agonist.

	Cetirizine crosses the blood-brain barrier only slightly, reducing the sedative side-effect common with older antihistamines. It has also been shown to inhibit eosinophil chemotaxis and LTB4 release. At a dosage of 20 mg, Boone et al. found that it inhibited the expression of VCAM-1 in patients with atopic dermatitis.
Cromoglicic acid	Cromoglicic acid (INN) (also referred to as cromolyn (USAN), cromoglycate (former BAN), or cromoglicate) is traditionally described as a mast cell stabilizer, and is commonly marketed as the sodium salt sodium cromoglicate or cromolyn sodium. This drug prevents the release of inflammatory chemicals such as histamine from mast cells. Because of their convenience (and perceived safety), leukotriene receptor antagonists have largely replaced it as the non-corticosteroid treatment of choice in the treatment of asthma.
Famciclovir	Famciclovir (INN) is a guanosine analogue antiviral drug used for the treatment of various herpesvirus infections, most commonly for herpes zoster (shingles). It is a prodrug form of penciclovir with improved oral bioavailability. Famciclovir is marketed under the trade name Famvir.
Glipizide	Glipizide is an oral rapid- and short-acting anti-diabetic drug from the sulfonylurea class. It is classified as a second generation sulfonylurea, which means that it undergoes enterohepatic circulation. Second-generation sulfonylureas are both more potent and have shorter half-lives than the first-generation sulfonylureas.
Glibenclamide	Glibenclamide (INN), also known as glyburide (USAN), is an antidiabetic drug in a class of medications known as sulfonylureas, closely related to sulfa drugs. It was developed in 1966 in a cooperative study between Boehringer Mannheim (now part of Roche) and Hoechst (now part of Sanofi-Aventis). It is sold in doses of 1.25 mg, 2.5 mg and 5 mg, under the trade names Diabeta, Glynase and Micronase in the United States and Daonil, Semi-Daonil and Euglucon in the United Kingdom and Delmide in India.
Hydrochlorothiazide	Hydrochlorothiazide, abbreviated HCTZ, HCT, or HZT, is a first-line diuretic drug of the thiazide class that acts by inhibiting the kidneys' ability to retain water. This reduces the volume of the blood, decreasing blood return to the heart and thus cardiac output and, by other mechanisms, is believed to lower peripheral vascular resistance. Hydrochlorothiazide is a calcium-sparing diuretic, meaning it can help the body get rid of excess water while still keeping calcium.
Insulin	Insulin is a peptide hormone, produced by beta cells of the pancreas, and is central to regulating carbohydrate and fat metabolism in the body. Insulin causes cells in the liver, skeletal muscles, and fat tissue to absorb glucose from the blood.

Metoprolol tartrate	Metoprolol is a selective β_1 receptor blocker used in treatment of several diseases of the cardiovascular system, especially hypertension. The active substance metoprolol is employed either as metoprolol succinate or metoprolol tartrate. The tartrate is an immediate-release and the succinate is an extended-release formulation.
Miconazole	Miconazole is an imidazole antifungal agent, developed by Janssen Pharmaceutica, commonly applied topically to the skin or to mucus membranes to cure fungal infections. It works by inhibiting the synthesis of ergosterol, a critical component of fungal cell membranes. It can also be used against certain species of Leishmania protozoa which are a type of unicellular parasite that also contain ergosterol in their cell membranes.
Ofloxacin	Ofloxacin is a synthetic chemotherapeutic antibiotic of the fluoroquinolone drug class considered to be a second-generation fluoroquinolone. The original brand, Floxin, has been discontinued by the manufacturer in the United States on 18 June 2009, though generic equivalents continue to be available. Ofloxacin was first patented in 1982 (European Patent Daiichi) and received approval from the U.S. Food and Drug Administration (FDA) on December 28, 1990. Ofloxacin is sold under a wide variety of brand names as well as generic drug equivalents, for oral and intravenous administration.
Omeprazole	Omeprazole is a proton pump inhibitor used in the treatment of dyspepsia, peptic ulcer disease (PUD), gastroesophageal reflux disease (GORD/GERD), laryngopharyngeal reflux (LPR) and Zollinger-Ellison syndrome. Omeprazole is one of the most widely prescribed drugs internationally and is available over the counter in some countries.
Paroxetine	Paroxetine is an antidepressant drug of the SSRI type. Paroxetine is used to treat major depression, obsessive-compulsive disorder, panic disorder, social anxiety, posttraumatic stress disorder and generalized anxiety disorder in adult outpatients. Marketing of the drug began in 1992 by the pharmaceutical company SmithKline Beecham, now GlaxoSmithKline.
Permethrin	Permethrin is a common synthetic chemical, widely used as an insecticide, acaricide, and insect repellent. It belongs to the family of synthetic chemicals called pyrethroids and functions as a neurotoxin, affecting neuron membranes by prolonging sodium channel activation. It is not known to rapidly harm most mammals or birds, but is dangerously toxic to cats and fish.
Prednisolone	Prednisolone is a synthetic glucocorticoid, a derivative of cortisol, which is used to treat a variety of inflammatory and auto-immune conditions. It is the active metabolite of the drug prednisone and is used especially in patients with hepatic failure, as these individuals are unable to metabolise prednisone into prednisolone.

2. UNIT-2 Pharmacokinetics and Pharmacodynamics,

Propranolol	Propranolol is a sympatholytic non-selective beta blocker. Sympatholytics are used to treat hypertension, anxiety and panic. It was the first successful beta blocker developed.
Ranitidine	Ranitidine is a histamine H_2-receptor antagonist that inhibits stomach acid production. It is commonly used in treatment of peptic ulcer disease (PUD) and gastroesophageal reflux disease (GERD). Ranitidine is also used alongside fexofenadine and other antihistamines for the treatment of skin conditions such as hives.
Salmeterol	Salmeterol is a long-acting beta2-adrenergic receptor agonist drug that is currently prescribed for the treatment of asthma and chronic obstructive pulmonary disease(COPD). It is currently available as a dry powder inhaler that releases a powdered form of the drug. Before 2008, it was also available as a metered-dose inhaler (MDI).
Tobramycin	Tobramycin is an aminoglycoside antibiotic derived from Streptomyces tenebrarius and used to treat various types of bacteria infections, particularly Gram-negative infections. It is especially effective against species of Pseudomonas.
Tretinoin	Tretinoin is the acid form of vitamin A and is also known as all-trans retinoic acid or ATRA. It is a first generation topical retinoid commonly used to treat acne vulgaris and keratosis pilaris. It is available as a cream or gel (brand names Aberela, Airol, Renova, Atralin, Retin-A, Avita, Retacnyl, Refissa, ReTrieve, or Stieva-A). It is also used to treat acute promyelocytic leukemia (APL), and is sold for this indication by Roche under the brand name Vesanoid.
Valacyclovir	Valaciclovir or valacyclovir is an antiviral drug used in the management of herpes simplex, herpes zoster (shingles), and herpes B. It is a prodrug, being converted in vivo to aciclovir. It is marketed by GlaxoSmithKline under the trade names Valtrex and Zelitrex. Valaciclovir has been available as a generic drug in the U.S. since November 25, 2009.
Zafirlukast	Zafirlukast is an oral leukotriene receptor antagonist (LTRA) for the maintenance treatment of asthma, often used in conjunction with an inhaled steroid and/or long-acting bronchodilator. It is available as a tablet and is usually dosed twice daily. Another leukotriene receptor antagonist is montelukast (Singulair), taken once daily. Zileuton (Zyflo), also used in the treatment of asthma via its inhibition of 5-lipoxygenase, is taken four times per day.
Lactation	Lactation describes the secretion of milk from the mammary glands and the period of time that a mother lactates to feed her young. The process occurs in all female mammals, although it predates mammals. In humans the process of feeding milk is called breastfeeding or nursing.
Sodium	Sodium is a chemical element with the symbol Na in the periodic table and atomic number 11. It is a soft, silvery-white, highly reactive metal and is a member of the alkali metals; its only stable isotope is ^{23}Na. The free metal does not occur in nature, but instead must be prepared from its compounds; it was first isolated by Humphry Davy in 1807 by the electrolysis of sodium hydroxide.

Alternative medicine	Alternative medicine is any of a wide range of health care practices, products and therapies, using methods of medical diagnosis and treatments which, at least up to the end of the twentieth century, were typically not included in the degree courses of established medical schools teaching western medicine, including surgery, in the tradition of the Flexner Report or similar. Examples include homeopathy, Ayurveda, chiropractic and acupuncture. Complementary medicine is alternative medicine used together with conventional medical treatment in a belief, not proven by using scientific methods, that it 'complements' the treatment.
Integrative medicine	Integrative medicine, which is also called integrated medicine and integrative health in the United Kingdom, combines alternative medicine with evidence-based medicine. Proponents claim that it treats the 'whole person,' focuses on wellness and health rather than on treating disease, and emphasizes the patient-physician relationship. Integrative medicine has been criticized for compromising the effectiveness of mainstream medicine through inclusion of ineffective alternative remedies, and for claiming it is distinctive in taking a rounded view of a person's health.
Traditional Chinese medicine	Traditional Chinese medicine is a broad range of medicine practices sharing common theoretical concepts which have been developed in China and are based on a tradition of more than 2,000 years, including various forms of herbal medicine, acupuncture, massage (Tui na), exercise (qigong), and dietary therapy. The doctrines of Chinese medicine are rooted in books such as the Yellow Emperor's Inner Canon and the Treatise on Cold Damage, as well as in cosmological notions like yin-yang and the five phases. Starting in the 1950s, these precepts were modernized in the People's Republic of China so as to integrate many anatomical and pathological notions with scientific medicine.
Echinacea	Echinacea is a genus of herbaceous flowering plants in the daisy family, Asteraceae. The nine species it contains are commonly called purple coneflowers. They are endemic to eastern and central North America, where they are found growing in moist to dry prairies and open wooded areas.
Melatonin	Melatonin , also known chemically as N-acetyl-5-methoxytryptamine, is a hormone found in animals, plants, and microbes. In animals, circulating levels of melatonin vary in a daily cycle, thereby allowing the entrainment of the circadian rhythms of several biological functions. Many biological effects of melatonin are produced through activation of melatonin receptors, while others are due to its role as a pervasive and powerful antioxidant, with a particular role in the protection of nuclear and mitochondrial DNA.

2. UNIT-2 Pharmacokinetics and Pharmacodynamics,

Kava	Kava-kava (Piper: Latin for 'pepper', methysticum: (Latinized) Greek for 'intoxicating') is a crop of the western Pacific. The name kava(-kava) is from Tongan and Marquesan; other names for kava include ?awa (Hawai?i), ava (Samoa), yaqona (Fiji), and sakau (Pohnpei). The roots of the plant are used to produce a drink with sedative and anesthetic properties.
Herbal medicine	Herbalism ('herbology' or 'herbal medicine') is use of plants for medicinal purposes, and the study of such use. Plants have been the basis for medical treatments through much of human history, and such traditional medicine is still widely practiced today. Modern medicine recognizes herbalism as a form of alternative medicine, as the practice of herbalism is not strictly based on evidence gathered using the scientific method.
Standardization	Standardization is the process of developing and implementing technical standards. The goals of right standardization can be to help with independence of single suppliers (commoditization), compatibility, interoperability, safety, repeatability, or quality. In social sciences, including economics, the idea of standardization is close to the solution for a coordination problem, a situation in which all parties can realize mutual gains, but only by making mutually consistent decisions.
Feverfew	Feverfew (Tanacetum parthenium; syn. Chrysanthemum parthenium (L). Pers., Pyrethrum parthenium Sm).
Green tea	Green tea is made from the leaves from Camellia sinensis that have undergone minimal oxidation during processing. Green tea originates in China, but it has become associated with many cultures throughout Asia. Green tea has recently become more widespread in the West, where black tea has been the traditionally consumed tea.
Comfrey	Comfrey is an important herb in organic gardening. It is used as a fertilizer and also has many purported medicinal uses. The main species used now is Symphytum ×?uplandicum or Russian comfrey, a hybrid between Symphytum officinale (common comfrey) and Symphytum asperum (rough comfrey).
Germander	Teucrium is a large genus of perennial plants in the family Lamiaceae. The name is believed to refer to King Teucer of Troy. Members of the genus are commonly known as germanders.
Lobelia	Lobelia is a genus of flowering plant comprising 360-400 species, with a subcosmopolitan distribution primarily in tropical to warm temperate regions of the world, a few species extending into cooler temperate regions. English names include Lobelia, Asthma Weed, Indian Tobacco, Pukeweed, and Vomitwort.

| Mandrake | Mandrake is the common name for members of the plant genus Mandragora belonging to the nightshades family (Solanaceae). Because mandrake contains deliriant hallucinogenic tropane alkaloids such as atropine, scopolamine, apoatropine, hyoscyamine and the roots sometimes contain bifurcations causing them to resemble human figures, their roots have long been used in magic rituals, today also in neopagan religions such as Wicca and Germanic revivalism religions such as Odinism.

Mandrake is also the common name of the plant species Mandragora officinarum, a plant which in Arabic is called luffâh, or beid el-jinn ('djinn's eggs'). |
| --- | --- |
| Yohimbe | Pausinystalia johimbe common name Yohimbe, is a plant species native to western and central Africa (Nigeria, Cabinda, Cameroon, Congo-Brazzaville, Gabon, Equatorial Guinea). The epithet 'johimbe' is often misspelled 'yohimbe' including by Beille in his 1906 recombination statement formally transferring the species from Corynanthe. Schumann's original 1901 description used the spelling 'johimbe,' and Beille clearly cited Schumann's name as basionym. |

1. _____ is a common synthetic chemical, widely used as an insecticide, acaricide, and insect repellent. It belongs to the family of synthetic chemicals called pyrethroids and functions as a neurotoxin, affecting neuron membranes by prolonging sodium channel activation. It is not known to rapidly harm most mammals or birds, but is dangerously toxic to cats and fish.

   a. Permethrin
   b. Propamidine
   c. Pyrantel pamoate
   d. Quinapyramine

2. . _____ is an alkaloid found in the nightshade family of plants (Solanaceae) that constitutes approximately 0.6-3.0% of the dry weight of tobacco, with biosynthesis taking place in the roots and accumulation occurring in the leaves. It functions as an antiherbivore chemical with particular specificity to insects; therefore _____ was widely used as an insecticide in the past, and currently _____ analogs such as imidacloprid continue to be widely used.

   In low concentrations (an average cigarette yields about 1 mg of absorbed _____), the substance acts as a stimulant in mammals and is the main factor responsible for the dependence-forming properties of tobacco smoking.

   a. PHA-543,613
   b. PNU-120,596
   c. PNU-282,987

2. UNIT-2 Pharmacokinetics and Pharmacodynamics,

3. _____ is a genus of flowering plant comprising 360-400 species, with a subcosmopolitan distribution primarily in tropical to warm temperate regions of the world, a few species extending into cooler temperate regions. English names include _____, Asthma Weed, Indian Tobacco, Pukeweed, and Vomitwort.

    Some botanists place the genus and its relatives in the separate family Lobeliaceae, others as a subfamily Lobelioideae within the Campanulaceae.

    a. Lobelia
    b. Lycopodium clavatum
    c. Malabathrum
    d. Manroot

4. In physiology and medicine, the _____ is the measured or calculated surface area of a human body. For many clinical purposes _____ is a better indicator of metabolic mass than body weight because it is less affected by abnormal adipose mass. Nevertheless, there have been several important critiques of the use of _____ in determining the dosage of medications with a narrow therapeutic index like many chemotherapy medications.

    a. drug metabolism
    b. Body surface area
    c. Sustained-release
    d. Homeopathic

5. _____ is the study of the biochemical and physiological effects of drugs on the body or on microorganisms or parasites within or on the body and the mechanisms of drug action and the relationship between drug concentration and effect. One dominant example is drug-receptor interactions as modeled by $L + R \rightleftharpoons L \cdot R$

    where L=ligand (drug), R=receptor (attachment site), reaction dynamics that can be studied mathematically through tools such as free energy maps. _____ is often summarized as the study of what a drug does to the body, whereas pharmacokinetics is the study of what the body does to a drug.

    a. Semisynthesis
    b. Pharmacodynamics
    c. Homeopathic
    d. isomer

ANSWER KEY
2. UNIT-2 Pharmacokinetics and Pharmacodynamics,

1. a
2. d
3. a
4. b
5. b

You can take the complete Online Interactive Chapter Practice Test

for 2. UNIT-2 Pharmacokinetics and Pharmacodynamics,
on all key terms, persons, places, and concepts.

No Additional Costs

http://www.Cram101.com

Register, send an email request to Travis.Reese@Cram101.com to get your user Id and password.

Include your customer order number, and ISBN number from your studyguide Retailer.

3. UNIT-3 The Art and Science of Pharmacotherapeutics,

CHAPTER OUTLINE: KEY TERMS, PEOPLE, PLACES, CONCEPTS

	Anticoagulant
	Prescription costs
	Substance abuse

CHAPTER HIGHLIGHTS & NOTES: KEY TERMS, PEOPLE, PLACES, CONCEPTS

Anticoagulant	An anticoagulant is a substance that prevents coagulation (clotting) of blood. Such substances occur naturally in leeches and blood-sucking insects. A group of pharmaceuticals called anticoagulants can be used in vivo as a medication for thrombotic disorders.
Prescription costs	Prescription costs are a common health care cost for many people and also the source of considerable economic hardship for some. These costs are sometimes referred to as out-of-pocket prescription costs, since for those with insurance, the total cost of their prescriptions may include expenses covered by a third party, such as an insurance company, as well as the individual. Out-of-pocket prescription costs include deductibles, co-payments, and upper limits in coverage.
Substance abuse	Substance abuse, is a patterned use of a substance (drug) in which the user consumes the substance in amounts or with methods neither approved nor advised by medical professionals. Substance abuse/drug abuse is not limited to mood-altering or psycho-active drugs. If an activity is performed using the objects against the rules and policies of the matter (as in steroids for performance enhancement in sports), it is also called substance abuse.

3. UNIT-3 The Art and Science of Pharmacotherapeutics,

1. _____, is a patterned use of a substance (drug) in which the user consumes the substance in amounts or with methods neither approved nor advised by medical professionals. _____/drug abuse is not limited to mood-altering or psycho-active drugs. If an activity is performed using the objects against the rules and policies of the matter (as in steroids for performance enhancement in sports), it is also called _____.

   a. hyperactivity disorder
   b. Restless leg
   c. Major depressive disorder
   d. Substance abuse

2. _____ are a common health care cost for many people and also the source of considerable economic hardship for some. These costs are sometimes referred to as out-of-pocket _____, since for those with insurance, the total cost of their prescriptions may include expenses covered by a third party, such as an insurance company, as well as the individual. Out-of-pocket _____ include deductibles, co-payments, and upper limits in coverage.

   a. PTC Therapeutics
   b. QS/1 Data Systems
   c. Quantum satis
   d. Prescription costs

3. An _____ is a substance that prevents coagulation (clotting) of blood. Such substances occur naturally in leeches and blood-sucking insects. A group of pharmaceuticals called _____s can be used in vivo as a medication for thrombotic disorders.

   a. Anticoagulant
   b. Apixaban
   c. Edoxaban
   d. Otamixaban

ANSWER KEY
3. UNIT-3 The Art and Science of Pharmacotherapeutics,

1. d
2. d
3. a

You can take the complete Online Interactive Chapter Practice Test

for 3. UNIT-3 The Art and Science of Pharmacotherapeutics,
on all key terms, persons, places, and concepts.

No Additional Costs

http://www.Cram101.com

Register, send an email request to Travis.Reese@Cram101.com to get your user Id and password.

Include your customer order number, and **ISBN** number from your studyguide Retailer.

4. UNIT-4 Topical Aaents,

CHAPTER OUTLINE: KEY TERMS, PEOPLE, PLACES, CONCEPTS

_____ | Aciclovir

_____ | Bacitracin

_____ | Benzoyl peroxide

_____ | Butenafine

_____ | Ciclopirox

_____ | Clindamycin

_____ | Crotamiton

_____ | Docosanol

_____ | Econazole

_____ | Gentamicin

_____ | Haloprogin

_____ | Ketoconazole

_____ | Lidocaine

_____ | Lindane

_____ | Malathion

_____ | Mepivacaine

_____ | Metronidazole

_____ | Mupirocin

_____ | Oxiconazole

_____ | Penciclovir

_____ | Pimecrolimus

Prilocaine

Sulconazole

Tacrolimus

Tolnaftate

Topical

Dermis

Subcutaneous tissue

Clobetasol propionate

Desonide

Fluocinonide

Fluticasone propionate

Halcinonide

Cortisol

Potency

Immunosuppressive drug

Polysporin

Pediculicide

Pharmacokinetics

Doxycycline

Salicylic acid

Azelaic acid

CHAPTER OUTLINE: KEY TERMS, PEOPLE, PLACES, CONCEPTS

Mechanism of action

Evening primrose

Gotu kola

Lavender

Olive leaf

Azelastine

Besifloxacin

Bimatoprost

Cyclosporine

Diclofenac

Dorzolamide

Fluorescein

Ganciclovir

Gatifloxacin

Ketorolac

Latanoprost

Levofloxacin

Lodoxamide

Moxifloxacin

Olopatadine

Proparacaine

_____ | Sulfacetamide _____

_____ | Allergic _____

_____ | Levocabastine _____

_____ | Naphazoline _____

_____ | Phenylephrine _____

_____ | Otitis media _____

CHAPTER HIGHLIGHTS & NOTES: KEY TERMS, PEOPLE, PLACES, CONCEPTS

Aciclovir	Aciclovir or acyclovir (USAN, former BAN), chemical name acycloguanosine, abbreviated as ACV, is a guanosine analogue antiviral drug, marketed under trade names such as Cyclovir, Herpex, Acivir, Acivirax, Zovirax, Zoral, and Xovir. One of the most commonly used antiviral drugs, it is primarily used for the treatment of herpes simplex virus infections, as well as in the treatment of varicella zoster (chickenpox) and herpes zoster (shingles). Aciclovir was seen as the start of a new era in antiviral therapy, as it is extremely selective and low in cytotoxicity.
Bacitracin	Bacitracin is a mixture of related cyclic polypeptides produced by organisms of the licheniformis group of Bacillus subtilis var Tracy, first isolated in 1945. These peptides disrupt both gram positive and gram negative bacteria by interfering with cell wall and peptidoglycan synthesis. Bacitracin is used as a topical preparation (since it is toxic and has poor oral bioavailability). In terms of adverse reactions only, in comparison with bacitracin, white petrolatum possesses an equally low infection rate and minimal risk for induction of allergy.
Benzoyl peroxide	Benzoyl peroxide is an organic compound in the peroxide family. It consists of two benzoyl groups bridged by a peroxide link. Its structural formula is $[C_6H_5C(O)]_2O_2$. It is one of the most important organic peroxides in terms of applications and the scale of its production. Benzoyl peroxide is used as an acne treatment, for improving flour, for bleaching hair and teeth, for polymerising polyester and many other uses.

4. UNIT-4 Topical Aaents,

CHAPTER HIGHLIGHTS & NOTES: KEY TERMS, PEOPLE, PLACES, CONCEPTS

Butenafine	Butenafine hydrochloride is a synthetic benzylamine antifungal, marketed under the trade names Mentax, Butop and is the active ingredient in Schering-Plough's Lotrimin Ultra. It is structurally related to synthetic allylamine antifungals such as terbinafine.
Ciclopirox	Ciclopirox olamine is a synthetic antifungal agent for topical dermatologic treatment of superficial mycoses. It is most useful against Tinea versicolor.
Clindamycin	Clindamycin rINN is a lincosamide antibiotic. It is usually used to treat infections with anaerobic bacteria, but can also be used to treat some protozoal diseases, such as malaria. It is a common topical treatment for acne and can be useful against some methicillin-resistant Staphylococcus aureus (MRSA) infections.
Crotamiton	Crotamiton is a drug that is used both as a scabicidal and as a general antipruritic (anti-itching drug). It is a prescription lotion based medicine that is applied to the whole body to get rid of the scabies parasite that burrows under the skin and causes itching.
Docosanol	Docosanol, also known as behenyl alcohol, is a saturated fatty alcohol used traditionally as an emollient, emulsifier, and thickener in cosmetics, nutritional supplement, and more recently, in a Food and Drug Administration (FDA) approved pharmaceutical, Abreva, approved as an antiviral agent for reducing the duration of cold sores caused by the herpes simplex virus. People who are allergic to one of the ingredients of Abreva are advised to avoid taking this medication. Also, it is not to be used by individuals who suffer from different medical conditions before consulting their health care provider.
Econazole	Econazole nitrate is an antifungal medication of the imidazole class. It is used as a cream under the brand names Spectazole (United States), Ecostatin (Canada), Pevaryl (Western Europe) and Pevisone (the latter consisting of the combination econazole/triamcinolone) to treat skin infections such as athlete's foot, tinea, pityriasis versicolor, ringworm, and jock itch. It is also sold in Canada under the brand name Ecostatin Vaginal Ovules to treat vaginal thrush.
Gentamicin	Gentamicin is an aminoglycoside antibiotic, used to treat many types of bacterial infections, particularly those caused by Gram-negative organisms. However, gentamicin is not used for Neisseria gonorrhoeae, Neisseria meningitidis or Legionella pneumophila. Gentamicin is also ototoxic and nephrotoxic, with this toxicity remaining a major problem in clinical use.
Haloprogin	Haloprogin is an antifungal drug used to treat athlete's foot and other fungal infections. It is marketed in creams under the trade names Halotex, Mycanden, Mycilan, and Polik.
Ketoconazole	Ketoconazole is a synthetic antifungal drug used to prevent and treat fungal skin infections, especially in immunocompromised patients such as those with AIDS or those on chemotherapy. Ketoconazole is sold commercially as an anti-dandruff shampoo, topical cream, and oral tablet.

4. UNIT-4 Topical Aaents,

Lidocaine	Lidocaine, xylocaine, or lignocaine (former BAN) is a common local anesthetic and antiarrhythmic drug. Lidocaine is used topically to relieve itching, burning and pain from skin inflammations, injected as a dental anesthetic or as a local anesthetic for minor surgery.
Lindane	Lindane, also known as gamma-hexachlorocyclohexane, (γ-HCH), gammaxene, Gammallin and erroneously known as benzene hexachloride (BHC), is an organochlorine chemical variant of hexachlorocyclohexane that has been used both as an agricultural insecticide and as a pharmaceutical treatment for lice and scabies.
	Lindane is a neurotoxin that interferes with GABA neurotransmitter function by interacting with the $GABA_A$ receptor-chloride channel complex at the picrotoxin binding site. In humans, lindane affects the nervous system, liver and kidneys, and may be a carcinogen.
Malathion	Malathion is an organophosphate parasympathomimetic which binds irreversibly to cholinesterase. Malathion is an insecticide of relatively low human toxicity. In the former USSR, it was known as carbophos, in New Zealand and Australia as maldison and in South Africa as mercaptothion.
Mepivacaine	Mepivacaine is a local anesthetic of the amide type. Mepivacaine has a reasonably rapid onset (more rapid than that of procaine) and medium duration of action (shorter than that of procaine) and is marketed under various trade names including Carbocaine and Polocaine.
	Mepivacaine became available in the United States in the 1960s.
Metronidazole	Metronidazole (INN) (Flagyl, and others) is a nitroimidazole antibiotic medication used particularly for anaerobic bacteria and protozoa. Metronidazole is an antibiotic, amebicide, and antiprotozoal. It is the drug of choice for first episodes of mild-to-moderate Clostridium difficile infection.
Mupirocin	Mupirocin is an antibiotic of the monoxycarbolic acid class. It was originally isolated from Pseudomonas fluorescens NCIMB 10586, developed by Beecham.
	Mupirocin is bacteriostatic at low concentrations and bactericidal at high concentrations. It is used topically and is effective against Gram-positive bacteria, including MRSA. Mupirocin is a mixture of several pseudomonic acids, with pseudomonic acid A (PA-A) constituting greater than 90% of the mixture. Also present in mupirocin are pseudomonic acid B with an additional hydroxyl group at C8, pseudomonic acid C with a double bond between C10 and C11, instead of the epoxide of PA-A, and pseudomonic acid D with a double bond at C4` and C5` in the 9-hydroxy-nonanoic acid portion of mupirocin.
Oxiconazole	Oxiconazole nitrate is an antifungal medication typically administered in a cream or lotion to treat skin infections, such as athlete's foot, jock itch and ringworm. It can also be prescribed to treat the skin rash known as tinea versicolor, caused by systemic yeast overgrowth (Candida spp)..

Mixich, G.; Thiele, K.; 1986, U.S. Patent 4,550,175.

Penciclovir	Penciclovir ( ) is a guanine analogue antiviral drug used for the treatment of various herpesvirus infections. It is a nucleoside analogue which exhibits low toxicity and good selectivity. Because penciclovir is absorbed poorly when given orally (by mouth) it is used more as a topical treatment, and is the active ingredient in the cold sore medications Denavir (NDC 0135-0315-52), Vectavir and Fenistil.
Pimecrolimus	Pimecrolimus is an immunomodulating agent used in the treatment of atopic dermatitis . It is available as a topical cream, once marketed by Novartis (however, Galderma has been promoting the compound in Canada since early 2007) under the trade name Elidel. See also: Immunomodulators in the treatment of eczema In January 2006, the United States Food and Drug Administration (FDA) announced that Elidel packaging would be required to carry a black box warning regarding the potential increased risk of lymph node or skin malignancy, as for the similar drug tacrolimus.
Prilocaine	Prilocaine is a local anesthetic of the amino amide type first prepared by Claes Tegner and Nils Löfgren. In its injectable form (trade name Citanest), it is often used in dentistry. It is also often combined with lidocaine as a preparation for dermal anesthesia (lidocaine/prilocaine or EMLA), for treatment of conditions like paresthesia.
Sulconazole	Sulconazole nitrate (trade name Exelderm) is an antifungal medication of the imidazole class. It is available as a cream or solution to treat skin infections such as athlete's foot, ringworm, jock itch, and sun fungus.
Tacrolimus	Tacrolimus is an immunosuppressive drug that is mainly used after allogeneic organ transplant to reduce the activity of the patient's immune system and so lower the risk of organ rejection. It is also used in a topical preparation in the treatment of atopic dermatitis (eczema), severe refractory uveitis after bone marrow transplants, exacerbations of minimal change disease, and the skin condition vitiligo. It is a 23-membered macrolide lactone discovered in 1984 from the fermentation broth of a Japanese soil sample that contained the bacteria Streptomyces tsukubaensis.
Tolnaftate	Tolnaftate is a synthetic over-the-counter anti-fungal agent. It may come as a cream, powder, spray, or liquid aerosol, and is used to treat jock itch, athlete's foot and ringworm. It is sold under several brand names, most notably Tinactin (Merck) and Odor Eaters (Combe Incorporated).

4. UNIT-4 Topical Aaents,

Topical	In medicine, a topical medication is applied to body surfaces such as the skin or mucous membranes such as the vagina, anus, throat, eyes and ears. Many topical medications are epicutaneous, meaning that they are applied directly to the skin. Topical medications may also be inhalational, such as asthma medications, or applied to the surface of tissues other than the skin, such as eye drops applied to the conjunctiva, or ear drops placed in the ear, or medications applied to the surface of a tooth.
Dermis	The dermis is a layer of skin between the epidermis and subcutaneous tissues, that consists of connective tissue and cushions the body from stress and strain. It is divided into two layers, the superficial area adjacent to the epidermis called the papillary region and a deep thicker area known as the reticular dermis. The dermis is tightly connected to the epidermis through a basement membrane.
Subcutaneous tissue	The hypodermis, also called the hypoderm, subcutaneous tissue, subcutis, or superficial fascia, is the lowermost layer of the integumentary system in vertebrates. Hypoderm and subcutaneous are from Greek and Latin words, respectively, for 'beneath the skin.' Types of cells that are found in the hypodermis are fibroblasts, adipose cells, and macrophages. It is derived from the mesoderm, but unlike the dermis, it is not derived from the dermatome region of the mesoderm.
Clobetasol propionate	Clobetasol propionate is a corticosteroid used to treat various skin disorders including eczema and psoriasis. It is also highly effective for contact dermatitis caused by exposure to poison ivy/oak. Clobetasol belongs to US Class I (Europe: class IV) of the corticosteroids, making it one of the most potent available.
Desonide	Desonide is the generic name of a low-potency topical corticosteroid that has been available since the 1970s. It is primarily used to treat atopic dermatitis (eczema), seborrheic dermatitis, contact dermatitis and psoriasis in both adults and children. It has a fairly good safety profile and is available as a cream, ointment, lotion, and as a foam under the tradename Verdeso Foam.
Fluocinonide	Fluocinonide (Fluonex, Lidex, Lidex-E, Lonide, Lyderm, and Vanos) is a potent glucocorticoid steroid used topically as an anti-inflammatory agent for the treatment of skin disorders such as eczema and seborrhoeic dermatitis. It relieves itching, redness, dryness, crusting, scaling, inflammation, and discomfort. The usual prescription concentration is 0.05% as a topical cream, ointment, or gel.
Fluticasone propionate	Fluticasone propionate is a corticosteroid derived from fluticasone used to treat asthma and allergic rhinitis (hay fever). It is also used to treat eosinophilic esophagitis.

Halcinonide	Halcinonide is a corticosteroid. It is used topically in the treatment of certain skin conditions.
Cortisol	Cortisol, known more formally as hydrocortisone is a steroid hormone, more specifically a glucocorticoid, produced by the zona fasciculata of the adrenal cortex. It is released in response to stress and a low level of blood glucocorticoids. Its primary functions are to increase blood sugar through gluconeogenesis; suppress the immune system; and aid in fat, protein and carbohydrate metabolism.
Potency	In the field of pharmacology, potency is a measure of drug activity expressed in terms of the amount required to produce an effect of given intensity. A highly potent drug (e.g., morphine, alprazolam, chlorpromazine) evokes a larger response at low concentrations, while a drug of lower potency evokes a small response at low concentrations. It is proportional to affinity and efficacy.
Immunosuppressive drug	Immunosuppressive drugs or immunosuppressive agents are drugs that inhibit or prevent activity of the immune system. They are used in immunosuppressive therapy to:•Prevent the rejection of transplanted organs and tissues (e.g., bone marrow, heart, kidney, liver)•Treat autoimmune diseases or diseases that are most likely of autoimmune origin (e.g., rheumatoid arthritis, multiple sclerosis, myasthenia gravis, systemic lupus erythematosus, sarcoidosis, focal segmental glomerulosclerosis, Crohn's disease, Behcet's Disease, pemphigus, and ulcerative colitis)•Treat some other non-autoimmune inflammatory diseases (e.g., long term allergic asthma control)
	A common side-effect of many immunosuppressive drugs is immunodeficiency, because the majority of them act non-selectively, resulting in increased susceptibility to infections and decreased cancer immunosurveillance. There are also other side-effects, such as hypertension, dyslipidemia, hyperglycemia, peptic ulcers, lipodystrophy, moon face, liver and kidney injury.
Polysporin	Polysporin is a line of antibiotic ointments produced by Johnson & Johnson used in the prevention of infection and speeding the healing of wounds. The original formulation contains bacitracin and polymyxin B.
	In the United States, Polysporin is less popular than Neosporin which contains a third antibiotic, neomycin. In Canada, the 'complete' version of Polysporin, which is known generically as 'triple antibioitic ointment', contains gramicidin as the third antibiotic, and does not contain neomycin.
Pediculicide	Pediculicides are substances used to treat lice .
Pharmacokinetics	Pharmacokinetics, is a branch of pharmacology dedicated to the determination of the fate of substances administered externally to a living organism. The substances of interest include pharmaceutical agents, hormones, nutrients, and toxins.
	Pharmacokinetics includes the study of the mechanisms of absorption and distribution of an administered drug, the chemical changes of the substance in the body (e.g.

4. UNIT-4 Topical Aaents,

Doxycycline	Doxycycline is a member of the tetracycline antibiotics group, and is commonly used to treat a variety of infections. Doxycycline is a semisynthetic tetracycline invented and clinically developed in the early 1960s by Pfizer Inc. and marketed under the brand name Vibramycin.
Salicylic acid	Salicylic acid is a monohydroxybenzoic acid, a type of phenolic acid and a beta hydroxy acid. This colorless crystalline organic acid is widely used in organic synthesis and functions as a plant hormone. It is derived from the metabolism of salicin.
Azelaic acid	Azelaic acid is an organic compound with the formula $(CH_2)_7(CO_2H)_2$. This saturated dicarboxylic acid exists as a white powder. It is found in wheat, rye, and barley.
Mechanism of action	In pharmacology, the term mechanism of action refers to the specific biochemical interaction through which a drug substance produces its pharmacological effect. A mechanism of action usually includes mention of the specific molecular targets to which the drug binds, such as an enzyme or receptor. For example, the mechanism of action of aspirin involves irreversible inhibition of the enzyme cyclooxygenase, therefore suppressing the production of prostaglandins and thromboxanes, thereby reducing pain and inflammation.
Evening primrose	Oenothera is a genus of about 145 species of herbaceous flowering plants native to the Americas. It is the type genus of the family Onagraceae. Common names include evening primrose, suncups, and sundrops.
Gotu kola	Centella asiatica, commonly centella (thankuni in Bengali: ???????, gotu kola in Sinhala: ???????, mandukaparni in Sanskrit: ?????????, pegagan in Indonesian, sleuk tracheakkranh in Khmer: ?????????????????, ondelaga in Kannada: ??????, vallaarai in Tamil: ???????) is a small, herbaceous, annual plant of the family Mackinlayaceae or subfamily Mackinlayoideae of family Apiaceae, and is native to India, Sri Lanka, northern Australia, Indonesia, Iran, Malaysia, Melanesia, Philippines, Papua New Guinea, and other parts of Asia. It is used as a medicinal herb in Ayurvedic medicine, traditional African medicine, and traditional Chinese medicine. Botanical synonyms include Hydrocotyle asiatica L. and Trisanthus cochinchinensis Lour..
Lavender	The lavenders (Lavandula) are a genus of 39 species of flowering plants in the mint family, Lamiaceae. An Old World genus, distributed from Macaronesia (Cape Verde and Canary Islands and Madeira) across Africa, the Mediterranean, South-West Asia, Arabia, Western Iran and South-East India. It is thought the genus originated in Asia but is most diversified in its western distribution.
Olive leaf	Olive leaf is the leaf of the olive tree (Olea europaea). While olive oil is well known for its flavor and health benefits, the leaf has been used medicinally in various times and places.

Azelastine	Azelastine is a potent, second-generation, selective, histamine antagonist (histamine-H_1-receptor antagonist) manufactured by MedaPharma. According to the Allergic Rhinitis and its Impact on Asthma (ARIA) treatment guidelines, intranasal anti-histamines are recommended for the first line therapy of mild intermittent, moderate/severe intermittent and mild persistent rhinitis (new classification system for rhinitis). The chemical nomenclature of azelastine is (±)-1-(2H)-phthalazinone, 4-[(4-chlorophenyl) methyl]-2 -(hexahydro-1-methyl-1H-azepin-4-yl)-monohydrochloride.
Besifloxacin	Besifloxacin is a fourth-generation fluoroquinolone antibiotic. The marketed compound is besifloxacin hydrochloride. It was developed by SSP Co. Ltd., Japan, and designated SS734. SSP licensed U.S. and European rights to SS734 for ophthalmic use to InSite Vision Incorporated (OTCBB: INSV) in 2000. InSite Vision developed an eye drop formulation (ISV-403) and conducted preliminary clinical trials before selling the product and all rights to Bausch & Lomb in 2003.
Bimatoprost	Bimatoprost is a prostaglandin analog/prodrug used topically (as eye drops) to control the progression of glaucoma and in the management of ocular hypertension. It reduces intraocular pressure (IOP) by increasing the outflow of aqueous fluid from the eyes. In December 2008, the indication to lengthen eyelashes was approved by the U.S. Food and Drug Administration (FDA); the cosmetic formulation of bimatoprost is sold as Latisse .
Cyclosporine	Ciclosporin (INNBAN), cyclosporine cyclosporin (former BAN), or cyclosporin A (often shortened to CsA) is an immunosuppressant drug widely used in organ transplantation to prevent rejection. It reduces the activity of the immune system by interfering with the activity and growth of T cells. It was initially isolated from the fungus Tolypocladium inflatum (Beauveria nivea), found in a soil sample obtained in 1969 from Hardangervidda, Norway by Dr. Hans Peter Frey, a Sandoz biologist.
Diclofenac	Diclofenac is a nonsteroidal anti-inflammatory drug (NSAID) taken to reduce inflammation and as an analgesic reducing pain in certain conditions. The name is derived from its chemical name: 2-(2,6-dichloranilino) phenylacetic acid. Diclofenac is used to treat pain, inflammatory disorders, and dysmenorrhea.
Dorzolamide	Dorzolamide is a carbonic anhydrase inhibitor. It is an anti-glaucoma agent by decreasing the production of aqueous humour. It is optically applied in the form of eye drops.
Fluorescein	Fluorescein is a synthetic organic compound available as a dark orange/red powder soluble in water and alcohol. It is widely used as a fluorescent tracer for many applications.

4. UNIT-4 Topical Aaents,

Ganciclovir	Ganciclovir INN ( ) is an antiviral medication used to treat or prevent cytomegalovirus (CMV) infections.Ganciclovir sodium is marketed under the trade names Cytovene and Cymevene (Roche). Ganciclovir for ocular use is marketed under the trade name Vitrasert (Bausch & Lomb). A prodrug form with improved oral bioavailability (valganciclovir) has also been developed.
Gatifloxacin	Gatifloxacin sold under the brand names Gatiflo, Tequin and Zymar, is an antibiotic of the fourth-generation fluoroquinolone family, that like other members of that family, inhibits the bacterial enzymes DNA gyrase and topoisomerase IV. Bristol-Myers Squibb introduced Gatifloxacin in 1999 under the proprietary name Tequin for the treatment of respiratory tract infections, having licensed the medication from Kyorin Pharmaceutical Company of Japan. Allergan produces an eye-drop formulation called Zymar. In many countries, gatifloxacin is also available as tablets and in various aqueous solutions for intravenous therapy.
Ketorolac	Ketorolac or ketorolac tromethamine is a non-steroidal anti-inflammatory drug (NSAID) in the family of heterocyclic acetic acid derivatives, often used as an analgesic. Ketorolac was discovered in 1989 by Syntex Corp. (now Roche Bioscience, which is a wholly owned subsidary of Roche holding Ltd., the parent company of Roche).
Latanoprost	Latanoprost ophthalmic solution is a medication administered into the eyes to control the progression of glaucoma or ocular hypertension by reducing intraocular pressure. It is a prostaglandin analogue (more specifically an analogue of prostaglandin F_{2a}) that lowers the pressure by increasing the outflow of aqueous fluid from the eyes through the uvealsclearal tract. Latanoprost is an isopropyl ester prodrug, meaning it is inactive until it is hydrolyzed by esterases in the cornea to the biologically active acid.
Levofloxacin	Levofloxacin (Levaquin., Tavanic (E.U)., and others) is a broad spectrum antibiotic of the fluoroquinolone drug class. Its spectrum of activity includes most strains of bacterial pathogens responsible for respiratory, urinary tract, gastrointestinal, and abdominal infections, including Gram-(-) (Escherichia coli, Haemophilus influenzae, Klebsiella pneumoniae, Legionella pneumophila, Moraxella catarrhalis, Proteus mirabilis, and Pseudomonas aeruginosa), Gram-(+) (methicillin-sensitive but not methicillin-resistant Staphylococcus aureus, Streptococcus pneumoniae, Staphylococcus epidermidis, Enterococcus faecalis, and Streptococcus pyogenes), and atypical bacterial pathogens (Chlamydophila pneumoniae and Mycoplasma pneumoniae). Levofloxacin and other fluoroquinolones are valued for this broad spectrum of activity, excellent tissue penetration, and for their availability in both oral and intravenous formulations.
Lodoxamide	Lodoxamide is an antiallergic. It resembles sodium cromoglycate in action as a mast cell stabilizer.
Moxifloxacin	Moxifloxacin is a fourth-generation synthetic fluoroquinolone antibacterial agent developed by Bayer AG (initially called BAY 12-8039). It is marketed worldwide (as the hydrochloride) under the brand names Avelox, Avalox, and Avelon for oral treatment.

4. UNIT-4 Topical Aaents,

Olopatadine	Olopatadine hydrochloride is an antihistamine, sold as a prescription eye drop (0.2% solution, Pataday (or Patanol S in some countries), manufactured by Alcon). It is used to treat itching associated with allergic conjunctivitis (eye allergies). Olopatadine hydrochloride 0.1% is sold as Patanol (or Opatanol in some countries).
Proparacaine	Proxymetacaine or proparacaine is a topical anesthetic drug of the aminoester group.
Sulfacetamide	Sulfacetamide is a sulfonamide antibiotic.
Allergic	An allergy is a hypersensitivity disorder of the immune system. Allergic reactions occur when a person's immune system reacts to normally harmless substances in the environment. A substance that causes a reaction is called an allergen.
Levocabastine	Levocabastine is a selective second-generation H_1-receptor antagonist which was discovered at Janssen Pharmaceutica in 1979. It is used for allergic conjunctivitis. As well as acting as an antihistamine, levocabastine has also subsequently been found to act as a potent and selective antagonist for the neurotensin receptor NTS_2, and was the first drug used to characterise the different neurotensin subtypes. This has made it a useful tool for the study of this receptor.
Naphazoline	Naphazoline is the common name for 2-(1-naphthylmethyl)-2-imidazoline hydrochloride. It is a sympathomimetic agent with marked alpha adrenergic activity. It is a vasoconstrictor with a rapid action in reducing swelling when applied to mucous membrane.
Phenylephrine	Phenylephrine is a selective a_1-adrenergic receptor agonist used primarily as a decongestant, as an agent to dilate the pupil, and to increase blood pressure. Phenylephrine is marketed as a substitute for the decongestant pseudoephedrine, though clinical studies differ regarding phenylephrine's effectiveness in this role.
Otitis media	Otitis media is the medical term for middle-ear inflammation. There are 2 major types of otitis media: acute otitis media and otitis media with effusion. The former is usually symptomatic, especially ear pain (otalgia), whereas the latter is most commonly without acute symptoms.

4. UNIT-4 Topical Aaents,

1. _____ is an antifungal drug used to treat athlete's foot and other fungal infections. It is marketed in creams under the trade names Halotex, Mycanden, Mycilan, and Polik.

   a. Hamycin
   b. Hexaconazole
   c. Ketoconazole
   d. Haloprogin

2. _____ or acyclovir (USAN, former BAN), chemical name acycloguanosine, abbreviated as ACV, is a guanosine analogue antiviral drug, marketed under trade names such as Cyclovir, Herpex, Acivir, Acivirax, Zovirax, Zoral, and Xovir. One of the most commonly used antiviral drugs, it is primarily used for the treatment of herpes simplex virus infections, as well as in the treatment of varicella zoster (chickenpox) and herpes zoster (shingles).

   _____ was seen as the start of a new era in antiviral therapy, as it is extremely selective and low in cytotoxicity.

   a. Adrenalin
   b. Albenza
   c. Aciclovir
   d. Allopurinol

3. _____ is a corticosteroid. It is used topically in the treatment of certain skin conditions.

   a. Halometasone
   b. Halcinonide
   c. Loteprednol
   d. Mineralocorticoid

4. _____ (INN) (Flagyl, and others) is a nitroimidazole antibiotic medication used particularly for anaerobic bacteria and protozoa. _____ is an antibiotic, amebicide, and antiprotozoal. It is the drug of choice for first episodes of mild-to-moderate Clostridium difficile infection.

   a. Metronidazole
   b. Famciclovir
   c. Piroxicam
   d. Pontocaine

5. . _____ is an aminoglycoside antibiotic, used to treat many types of bacterial infections, particularly those caused by Gram-negative organisms. However, _____ is not used for Neisseria gonorrhoeae, Neisseria meningitidis or Legionella pneumophila. _____ is also ototoxic and nephrotoxic, with this toxicity remaining a major problem in clinical use.

   a. Gentamicin
   b. Griseofulvin
   c. Halothane

1. d

2. c

3. b

4. a

5. a

You can take the complete Online Interactive Chapter Practice Test

for 4. UNIT-4 Topical Aaents,
on all key terms, persons, places, and concepts.

No Additional Costs

http://www.Cram101.com

Register, send an email request to Travis.Reese@Cram101.com to get your user Id and password.

Include your customer order number, and ISBN number from your studyguide Retailer.

5. UNIT-5 Respiratory Agents,

CHAPTER OUTLINE: KEY TERMS, PEOPLE, PLACES, CONCEPTS

Benzonatate

Diphenhydramine

Loratadine

Oxymetazoline

Topical

Mechanism of action

Acrivastine

Hydrocodone

Pharmacokinetics

Cromoglicic acid

Pseudoephedrine

Codeine sulfate

Beclomethasone

Budesonide

Ipratropium bromide

Methylprednisolone

Pirbuterol

Tiotropium bromide

Asthma

Pulmonary function

Inflammation

	Tiotropium
	Inhaler
	Chronic obstructive pulmonary disease
	Formoterol
	Bitolterol

CHAPTER HIGHLIGHTS & NOTES: KEY TERMS, PEOPLE, PLACES, CONCEPTS

Benzonatate	Benzonatate is a non-narcotic oral cough suppressant, or antitussive, with effects that last from 6 to 8 hours. Its formal name is 2,5,8,11,14,17,20,23,26-nonaoxaoctacosan-28-yl para-butylaminobenzoate. Since it is not an opioid, benzonatate is not prone to abuse like some other cough medications such as codeine.
Diphenhydramine	Diphenhydramine is a first-generation antihistamine possessing anticholinergic, antitussive, antiemetic, and sedative properties that is mainly used to treat allergies. It is also used in the management of drug-induced parkinsonism and other extrapyramidal symptoms. The drug has a strong hypnotic effect and is FDA-approved as a non-prescription sleep aid, especially in the form of diphenhydramine citrate.
Loratadine	Loratadine (INN) is a second-generation H_1 histamine antagonist drug used to treat allergies. Structurally, it is closely related to tricyclic antidepressants, such as imipramine, and is distantly related to the atypical antipsychotic quetiapine. Loratadine is marketed by Schering-Plough under several trade names (e.g., Claritin) and also by Shionogi in Japan. It is available as a generic drug and is marketed for its non-sedating properties. In a version named Claritin-D or Clarinase, it is combined with pseudoephedrine, a decongestant; this makes it useful for colds as well as allergies but adds potential side-effects of insomnia, anxiety, and nervousness.
Oxymetazoline	Oxymetazoline is a selective alpha-1 agonist and partial alpha-2 agonist topical decongestant, used in the form of Oxymetazoline hydrochloride, in products such as Afrin, Dristan, Nasivin, Logicin, Vicks Sinex, Visine L.R., Sudafed OM, and Zicam.

	It was developed from xylometazoline at E. Merck Darmstadt by Fruhstorfer in 1961. Oxymetazoline is generally available as a nasal spray.
Topical	In medicine, a topical medication is applied to body surfaces such as the skin or mucous membranes such as the vagina, anus, throat, eyes and ears. Many topical medications are epicutaneous, meaning that they are applied directly to the skin. Topical medications may also be inhalational, such as asthma medications, or applied to the surface of tissues other than the skin, such as eye drops applied to the conjunctiva, or ear drops placed in the ear, or medications applied to the surface of a tooth.
Mechanism of action	In pharmacology, the term mechanism of action refers to the specific biochemical interaction through which a drug substance produces its pharmacological effect. A mechanism of action usually includes mention of the specific molecular targets to which the drug binds, such as an enzyme or receptor. For example, the mechanism of action of aspirin involves irreversible inhibition of the enzyme cyclooxygenase, therefore suppressing the production of prostaglandins and thromboxanes, thereby reducing pain and inflammation.
Acrivastine	Acrivastine is a medication used for the treatment of allergies and hay fever. It is a second-generation H1-receptor antagonist antihistamine (like its base molecule triprolidine) and works by blocking Histamine H1 receptors. This non-sedating antihistamine is sold under the brand name Benadryl Allergy Relief in the U.K. by McNeil Laboratories, not to be confused with Benadryl Once a Day, which is cetirizine and is also sold by McNeil in the U.K. It is available as an over-the-counter medication in the UK. In the U.S., acrivastine is the active ingredient in the Semprex-D brand.
Hydrocodone	Hydrocodone is a synthetic opioid derived from either of two naturally occurring opiates: codeine and thebaine. It is an orally active narcotic analgesic (pain reliever) and antitussive (cough suppressant). It is available in tablet, capsule, and syrup form.
Pharmacokinetics	Pharmacokinetics, is a branch of pharmacology dedicated to the determination of the fate of substances administered externally to a living organism. The substances of interest include pharmaceutical agents, hormones, nutrients, and toxins. Pharmacokinetics includes the study of the mechanisms of absorption and distribution of an administered drug, the chemical changes of the substance in the body (e.g.

5. UNIT-5 Respiratory Agents,

Cromoglicic acid	Cromoglicic acid (INN) (also referred to as cromolyn (USAN), cromoglycate (former BAN), or cromoglicate) is traditionally described as a mast cell stabilizer, and is commonly marketed as the sodium salt sodium cromoglicate or cromolyn sodium. This drug prevents the release of inflammatory chemicals such as histamine from mast cells. Because of their convenience (and perceived safety), leukotriene receptor antagonists have largely replaced it as the non-corticosteroid treatment of choice in the treatment of asthma.
Pseudoephedrine	Pseudoephedrine is a sympathomimetic drug of the phenethylamine and amphetamine chemical classes. It may be used as a nasal/sinus decongestant, as a stimulant, or as a wakefulness-promoting agent. The salts pseudoephedrine hydrochloride and pseudoephedrine sulfate are found in many over-the-counter preparations, either as a single ingredient or (more commonly) in combination with antihistamines, guaifenesin, dextromethorphan, and/or paracetamol (acetaminophen) or another NSAID (such as aspirin or ibuprofen). Pseudoephedrine is a diastereomer of ephedrine and is readily reduced into methamphetamine or oxidized into methcathinone.
Codeine sulfate	Codeine or 3-methylmorphine is an opiate used for its analgesic, antitussive, antidiarrheal, antihypertensive, anxiolytic, antidepressant, sedative and hypnotic properties. It is also used to suppress premature labor contractions, myocardial infarction, and has many other potential and indicated uses. It is often sold as a salt in the form of either codeine sulfate or codeine phosphate in the United States and Canada; codeine hydrochloride is more common worldwide and the citrate, hydroiodide, hydrobromide, tartrate, and other salts are also seen.
Beclomethasone	Beclometasone dipropionate (INN modified) or beclomethasone dipropionate (USAN, former BAN) is a potent glucocorticoid steroid. It is a prodrug of the free form, beclometasone (INN). In the form of an inhaler (e.g. Clenil, Qvar), a wide number of brands of which are available, it is used for the prophylaxis of asthma.
Budesonide	Budesonide is a glucocorticoid steroid for the treatment of asthma and non-infectious rhinitis (including hay fever and other allergies), and for treatment and prevention of nasal polyposis. In addition, it is used for Crohn's disease (inflammatory bowel disease). It is marketed by AstraZeneca as a nasal inhalant under the brand name Rhinocort (in Denmark, as Rhinosol), as an oral inhalant under the brand name Pulmicort (in Israel, Budicort), and as either an enema or a modified-release oral capsule under the brand name Entocort.
Ipratropium bromide	Ipratropium bromide is an anticholinergic drug used for the treatment of chronic obstructive pulmonary disease and acute asthma. It blocks the muscarinic acetylcholine receptors in the smooth muscles of the bronchi in the lungs, opening the bronchi.

5. UNIT-5 Respiratory Agents,

Methylprednisolone	Methylprednisolone is a synthetic glucocorticoid or corticosteroid drug. It is marketed in the USA and Canada under the brand names Medrol and Solu-Medrol. It is also available as a generic drug.
Pirbuterol	Pirbuterol is a beta-2 adrenergic bronchodilator used in the treatment of asthma, available (as pirbuterol acetate) as a breath-activated metered-dose inhaler ('autohaler').
Tiotropium bromide	Tiotropium bromide is a long-acting, 24 hour, anticholinergic bronchodilator used in the management of chronic obstructive pulmonary disease (COPD).In India it is marketed by Intas under the trade name 'Quikhale T'. Tiotropium bromide capsules for inhalation are co-promoted by Boehringer-Ingelheim and Pfizer under the trade name Spiriva. It is also manufactured and marketed by Cipla under trade name Tiova.
Asthma	Asthma is a common chronic inflammatory disease of the airways characterized by variable and recurring symptoms, reversible airflow obstruction, and bronchospasm. Common symptoms include wheezing, coughing, chest tightness, and shortness of breath. Asthma is thought to be caused by a combination of genetic and environmental factors.
Pulmonary function	Pulmonary Function Testing is a complete evaluation of the respiratory system including patient history, physical examinations, chest x-ray examinations, arterial blood gas analysis, and tests of pulmonary function. The primary purpose of pulmonary function testing is to identify the severity of pulmonary impairment. Pulmonary function testing has diagnostic and therapeutic roles and helps clinicians answer some general questions about patients with lung disease.
Inflammation	Inflammation is part of the complex biological response of vascular tissues to harmful stimuli, such as pathogens, damaged cells, or irritants. The classical signs of acute inflammation are pain, heat, redness, swelling, and loss of function. Inflammation is a protective attempt by the organism to remove the injurious stimuli and to initiate the healing process.
Tiotropium	Tiotropium bromide (INN) is a long-acting, 24 hour, anticholinergic bronchodilator used in the management of chronic obstructive pulmonary disease (COPD).In India it is marketed by Intas under the trade name 'Quikhale T'. Tiotropium bromide capsules for inhalation are co-promoted by Boehringer-Ingelheim and Pfizer under the trade name Spiriva. It is also manufactured and marketed by Cipla under trade name Tiova.
Inhaler	An inhaler or puffer is a medical device used for delivering medication into the body via the lungs. It is mainly used in the treatment of asthma and Chronic Obstructive Pulmonary Disease (COPD). Zanamivir (Relenza), used to treat influenza, must be administered via inhaler.
Chronic obstructive pulmonary disease	Chronic obstructive pulmonary disease, also known as chronic obstructive lung disease (COLD), and chronic obstructive airway disease (COAD), among others, is a type of obstructive lung disease characterized by chronically poor airflow. It typically worsens over time.

5. UNIT-5 Respiratory Agents,

Formoterol	Formoterol or eformoterol is a long-acting β_2-agonist used in the management of asthma and/or chronic obstructive pulmonary disease (COPD). It is marketed in four forms: a dry-powder inhaler (DPI), a metered-dose inhaler (MDI), an oral tablet, and an inhalation solution, under various trade names including ForadilForadile (Schering-Plough in the U.S., Novartis rest of world), Oxeze/Oxis (AstraZeneca), Atock (Astellas), Atimos (Modulite) (Chiesi), and Perforomist (Dey). Formoterol is a long-acting β_2 agonist (LABA) that has an extended duration of action (up to 12 hours) compared to short-acting β_2 agonists such as salbutamol, which are effective for 4-6 hours.
Bitolterol	Bitolterol mesylate is a β_2-adrenergic receptor agonist used for the relief of bronchospasm in conditions such as asthma and COPD. In these disorders there is a narrowing of the airways (bronchi and their ramifications) that carry air to the lungs. Muscle spasm and inflammation within the bronchi get worse this narrowing. Bitolterol relaxes the smooth muscles present continuously around the bronchi and bronchioles facilitating the flow of air through them.

1. _____ (INN) is a second-generation H_1 histamine antagonist drug used to treat allergies. Structurally, it is closely related to tricyclic antidepressants, such as imipramine, and is distantly related to the atypical antipsychotic quetiapine.

   _____ is marketed by Schering-Plough under several trade names (e.g., Claritin) and also by Shionogi in Japan. It is available as a generic drug and is marketed for its non-sedating properties. In a version named Claritin-D or Clarinase, it is combined with pseudoephedrine, a decongestant; this makes it useful for colds as well as allergies but adds potential side-effects of insomnia, anxiety, and nervousness.

   a. Loratadine
   b. Homeopathic
   c. Chiropractic
   d. Pepto-Bismol

2. . _____ bromide (INN) is a long-acting, 24 hour, anticholinergic bronchodilator used in the management of chronic obstructive pulmonary disease (COPD).In India it is marketed by Intas under the trade name 'Quikhale T'. _____ bromide capsules for inhalation are co-promoted by Boehringer-Ingelheim and Pfizer under the trade name Spiriva. It is also manufactured and marketed by Cipla under trade name Tiova.

   a. Macugen
   b. Tiotropium

   c. Somavert

   d. Latanoprost

3. _____ is a non-narcotic oral cough suppressant, or antitussive, with effects that last from 6 to 8 hours. Its formal name is 2,5,8,11,14,17,20,23,26-nonaoxaoctacosan-28-yl para-butylaminobenzoate. Since it is not an opioid, _____ is not prone to abuse like some other cough medications such as codeine.

   a. Cantharidin

   b. Benzonatate

   c. Tioconazole

   d. Homeopathic

4. Beclometasone dipropionate (INN modified) or _____ dipropionate (USAN, former BAN) is a potent glucocorticoid steroid. It is a prodrug of the free form, beclometasone (INN). In the form of an inhaler (e.g. Clenil, Qvar), a wide number of brands of which are available, it is used for the prophylaxis of asthma.

   a. Homeopathic

   b. Beclomethasone

   c. Pepto-Bismol

   d. Flocoumafen

5. _____ is a sympathomimetic drug of the phenethylamine and amphetamine chemical classes. It may be used as a nasal/sinus decongestant, as a stimulant, or as a wakefulness-promoting agent.

The salts _____ hydrochloride and _____ sulfate are found in many over-the-counter preparations, either as a single ingredient or (more commonly) in combination with antihistamines, guaifenesin, dextromethorphan, and/or paracetamol (acetaminophen) or another NSAID (such as aspirin or ibuprofen). _____ is a diastereomer of ephedrine and is readily reduced into methamphetamine or oxidized into methcathinone.

   a. Pseudoephedrine

   b. Homeopathic

   c. Chiropractic

   d. Flocoumafen

ANSWER KEY
5. UNIT-5 Respiratory Agents,

1. a
2. b
3. b
4. b
5. a

You can take the complete Online Interactive Chapter Practice Test

for 5. UNIT-5 Respiratory Agents,
on all key terms, persons, places, and concepts.

No Additional Costs

http://www.Cram101.com

Register, send an email request to Travis.Reese@Cram101.com to get your user Id and password.

Include your customer order number, and ISBN number from your studyguide Retailer.

6. UNIT-6 Cardiovascular Agents,

CHAPTER OUTLINE: KEY TERMS, PEOPLE, PLACES, CONCEPTS

	Aliskiren
	Angiotensin-converting enzyme
	Antihypertensive
	Hydralazine
	Minoxidil
	Prazosin
	Hypertension
	Metabolic syndrome
	Mechanism of action
	Pharmacokinetics
	Isosorbide
	Ranolazine
	Risk factor
	Angina
	Lipoprotein
	Myocardial infarction
	Digoxin
	Glycosides
	Heart failure
	Toxicity
	Atenolol

CHAPTER OUTLINE: KEY TERMS, PEOPLE, PLACES, CONCEPTS

	Betaxolol
	Nebivolol
	Pindolol
	Hyperthyroidism
	Metoprolol
	Amlodipine
	Felodipine
	Nifedipine
	Nisoldipine
	Calcium channel blocker
	Benazepril
	Captopril
	Eprosartan
	Fosinopril
	Lisinopril
	Moexipril hydrochloride
	Perindopril
	Ramipril
	Valsartan
	Quinapril
	Renal failure

Angioedema

Adenosine

Dofetilide

Dronedarone

Flecainide

Ibutilide

Mexiletine

Procainamide

Quinidine

Tachycardia

Tocainide

Antiarrhythmic agent

Disopyramide

Cholestyramine

Ezetimibe

Fenofibrate

Gemfibrozil

Hyperlipidemia

Niacin

Nicotinic acid

Pitavastatin

CHAPTER OUTLINE: KEY TERMS, PEOPLE, PLACES, CONCEPTS

	Pravastatin
	Simvastatin
	Colestipol
	Red yeast rice
	Abciximab
	Anisindione
	Aspirin
	Clopidogrel
	Dalteparin
	Fondaparinux
	Streptokinase
	Ticlopidine
	Tinzaparin
	Warfarin
	Low molecular weight heparin
	Dabigatran
	Prasugrel
	Pulmonary embolism
	Vitamin K
	Heparin
	Stroke

6. UNIT-6 Cardiovascular Agents,

	Phosphodiesterase inhibitor
	Anticoagulant
	Cilostazol
	Enoxaparin

CHAPTER HIGHLIGHTS & NOTES: KEY TERMS, PEOPLE, PLACES, CONCEPTS

Aliskiren	Aliskiren (trade names Tekturna, US; Rasilez, UK and elsewhere) is the first in a class of drugs called direct renin inhibitors. Its current licensed indication is essential (primary) hypertension. Aliskiren was co-developed by the Swiss pharmaceutical companies Novartis and Speedel.
Angiotensin-converting enzyme	Angiotensin-converting enzyme, or 'Angiotensin converting enzyme' indirectly increases blood pressure by causing blood vessels to constrict. It does that by converting angiotensin I to angiotensin II, which constricts the vessels. For this reason, drugs known as Angiotensin converting enzyme inhibitors are used to lower blood pressure.
Antihypertensive	Antihypertensives are a class of drugs that are used to treat hypertension (high blood pressure). Antihypertensive therapy seeks to prevent the complications of high blood pressure, such as stroke and myocardial infarction. Evidence suggests that reduction of the blood pressure by 5 mmHg can decrease the risk of stroke by 34%, of ischaemic heart disease by 21%, and reduce the likelihood of dementia, heart failure, and mortality from cardiovascular disease.
Hydralazine	Hydralazine is a direct-acting smooth muscle relaxant used to treat hypertension by acting as a vasodilator primarily in arteries and arterioles. By relaxing vascular smooth muscle, vasodilators act to decrease peripheral resistance, thereby lowering blood pressure and decreasing afterload. However, this only has a short term effect on blood pressure, as the system will reset to the previous, high blood pressure necessary to maintain pressure in the kidney necessary for natriuresis.
Minoxidil	Minoxidil is an antihypertensive vasodilator medication which also slows or stops hair loss and promotes hair regrowth. Now off-patent, it is available over-the-counter for the treatment of androgenic alopecia.

Prazosin	Prazosin, trade names Minipress, Vasoflex, Pressin and Hypovase, is a sympatholytic drug used to treat high blood pressure and anxiety, PTSD, and panic disorder. It is an alpha-adrenergic blocker that is specific for the alpha-1 receptors. These receptors are found on vascular smooth muscle, where they are responsible for the vasoconstrictive action of norepinephrine.
Hypertension	Hypertension or high blood pressure, sometimes called arterial hypertension, is a chronic medical condition in which the blood pressure in the arteries is elevated. This requires the heart to work harder than normal to circulate blood through the blood vessels. Blood pressure is summarised by two measurements, systolic and diastolic, which depend on whether the heart muscle is contracting (systole) or relaxed between beats (diastole) and equate to a maximum and minimum pressure, respectively.
Metabolic syndrome	Metabolic syndrome is a disorder of energy utilization and storage, diagnosed by a co-occurrence of three out of five of the following medical conditions: abdominal obesity, elevated blood pressure, elevated fasting plasma glucose, high serum triglycerides, and low high-density cholesterol (HDL) levels. Metabolic syndrome increases the risk of developing cardiovascular disease, particularly heart failure, and diabetes. Some studies have shown the prevalence in the USA to be an estimated 34% of the adult population, and the prevalence increases with age.
Mechanism of action	In pharmacology, the term mechanism of action refers to the specific biochemical interaction through which a drug substance produces its pharmacological effect. A mechanism of action usually includes mention of the specific molecular targets to which the drug binds, such as an enzyme or receptor. For example, the mechanism of action of aspirin involves irreversible inhibition of the enzyme cyclooxygenase, therefore suppressing the production of prostaglandins and thromboxanes, thereby reducing pain and inflammation.
Pharmacokinetics	Pharmacokinetics, is a branch of pharmacology dedicated to the determination of the fate of substances administered externally to a living organism. The substances of interest include pharmaceutical agents, hormones, nutrients, and toxins. Pharmacokinetics includes the study of the mechanisms of absorption and distribution of an administered drug, the chemical changes of the substance in the body (e.g. by metabolic enzymes such as CYP or UGT enzymes), and the effects and routes of excretion of the metabolites of the drug.
Isosorbide	Isosorbide is a heterocyclic compound that is derived from glucose. Isosorbide and its two isomers, namely isoidide and isomannide, are 1,4:3,6-dianhydrohexitols. It is a white solid that is prepared from the double dehydration of sorbitol.

6. UNIT-6 Cardiovascular Agents,

Ranolazine	Ranolazine, sold under the trade name Ranexa by Gilead Sciences (who acquired the developer, CV Therapeutics in 2009), is an antianginal medication. In India, it is sold under the name 'Ranozex'. On January 31, 2006, ranolazine was approved for use in the United States by the FDA for the treatment of chronic angina pectoris.
Risk factor	In epidemiology, a risk factor is a variable associated with an increased risk of disease or infection. Sometimes, determinant is also used, being a variable associated with either increased or decreased risk.
Angina	Angina pectoris - commonly known as angina - is chest pain due to ischemia of the heart muscle, generally due to obstruction or spasm of the coronary arteries. The main cause of Angina pectoris is coronary artery disease, due to atherosclerosis of the arteries feeding the heart. The term derives from the Latin angina from the Greek ?γχ?νη ankhone ('strangling'), and the Latin pectus ('chest'), and can therefore be translated as 'a strangling feeling in the chest'.
Lipoprotein	A lipoprotein is a biochemical assembly that contains both proteins and lipids, bound to the proteins, which allow fats to move through the water inside and outside cells. The proteins serve to emulsify the lipid molecules. Many enzymes, transporters, structural proteins, antigens, adhesins, and toxins are lipoproteins.
Myocardial infarction	Myocardial infarction or acute myocardial infarction commonly known as a heart attack, results from the partial interruption of blood supply to a part of the heart muscle, causing the heart cells to be damaged or die. This is most commonly due to occlusion (blockage) of a coronary artery following the rupture of a vulnerable atherosclerotic plaque, which is an unstable collection of cholesterol and fatty acids and white blood cells in the wall of an artery. The resulting ischemia (restriction in blood supply) and ensuing oxygen shortage, if left untreated for a sufficient period of time, can cause damage or death (infarction) of heart muscle tissue (myocardium).
Digoxin	Digoxin INN is a purified cardiac glycoside extracted from the foxglove plant, Digitalis lanata, which was discovered by William Withering. Its corresponding aglycone is digoxigenin, and its acetyl derivative is acetyldigoxin. Digoxin is widely used in the treatment of various heart conditions, namely atrial fibrillation, atrial flutter and sometimes heart failure that cannot be controlled by other medication.
Glycosides	In chemistry, a glycoside is a molecule in which a sugar is bound to a non-carbohydrate moiety, usually a small organic molecule. Glycosides play numerous important roles in living organisms. Many plants store chemicals in the form of inactive glycosides.
Heart failure	Heart failure often called congestive heart failure or congestive cardiac failure (CCF), occurs when the heart is unable to provide sufficient pump action to maintain blood flow to meet the needs of the body. Heart failure can cause a number of symptoms including shortness of breath, leg swelling, and exercise intolerance.

Toxicity	Toxicity is the degree to which a substance can damage an organism. Toxicity can refer to the effect on a whole organism, such as an animal, bacterium, or plant, as well as the effect on a substructure of the organism, such as a cell (cytotoxicity) or an organ such as the liver (hepatotoxicity). By extension, the word may be metaphorically used to describe toxic effects on larger and more complex groups, such as the family unit or society at large.
Atenolol	Atenolol is a selective β_1 receptor antagonist, a drug belonging to the group of beta blockers, a class of drugs used primarily in cardiovascular diseases. Introduced in 1976, atenolol was developed as a replacement for propranolol in the treatment of hypertension. The chemical works by slowing down the heart and reducing its workload.
Betaxolol	Betaxolol is a selective $beta_1$ receptor blocker used in the treatment of hypertension and glaucoma. Being selective for $beta_1$ receptors, it typically has fewer systemic side effects than non-selective beta-blockers, for example, not causing bronchospasm (mediated by $beta_2$ receptors) as timolol may. Betaxolol also shows greater affininty for $beta_1$ receptors than metoprolol.
Nebivolol	Nebivolol is a $ß_1$ receptor blocker with nitric oxide-potentiating vasodilatory effect used in treatment of hypertension and, in Europe, also for left ventricular failure. It is highly cardioselective under certain circumstances.
Pindolol	Pindolol is a beta blocker.
Hyperthyroidism	Hyperthyroidism, is a condition in which the thyroid gland produces and secretes excessive amounts of the free thyroid hormones, triiodothyronine (T3) and/or thyroxine (T4). This is the opposite of hypothyroidism ('sluggish thyroid'), which is the reduced production and secretion of T3 and/or T4. Hyperthyroidism is a type of thyrotoxicosis, a hypermetabolic clinical syndrome which occurs when there are elevated serum levels of T3 and/or T4. Graves' disease is the most common cause of hyperthyroidism.

While hyperthyroidism may cause thyrotoxicosis they are not synonymous medical conditions; some patients may develop thyrotoxicosis as a result of inflammation of the thyroid gland (thyroiditis), which may cause the release of excessive thyroid hormone already stored in the gland but does not cause accelerated hormone production. |
| Metoprolol | Metoprolol is a selective β_1 receptor blocker used in treatment of several diseases of the cardiovascular system, especially hypertension. The active substance metoprolol is employed either as metoprolol succinate or metoprolol tartrate (where 100 mg metoprolol tartrate corresponds to 95 mg metoprolol succinate). The tartrate is an immediate-release and the succinate is an extended-release formulation. |

6. UNIT-6 Cardiovascular Agents,

Amlodipine	Amlodipine (as besylate, mesylate or maleate) is a long-acting calcium channel blocker dihydropyridine (DHP) class used as an antihypertensive and in the treatment of angina pectoris. Like other calcium channel blockers, amlodipine acts by relaxing the smooth muscle in the arterial wall, decreasing total peripheral resistance thereby reducing blood pressure; in angina, amlodipine increases blood flow to the heart muscle (although DHP-class calcium channel blockers are more selective for arteries than the muscular tissue of the heart (myocardium), as the cardiac calcium channels are not of the dihydropyridine-type).
Felodipine	Felodipine is a calcium channel blocker (calcium antagonist), a drug used to control hypertension (high blood pressure). It is marketed under the brand name Plendil by AstraZeneca and Renedil by Sanofi-Aventis. The formulation patent for the substance expired in 2007.
Nifedipine	Nifedipine is a dihydropyridine calcium channel blocker. Its main uses are as an antianginal (especially in Prinzmetal's angina) and antihypertensive, although a large number of other indications have recently been found for this agent, such as Raynaud's phenomenon, premature labor, and painful spasms of the esophagus in cancer and tetanus patients. It is also commonly used for the small subset of pulmonary hypertension patients whose symptoms respond to calcium channel blockers.
Nisoldipine	Nisoldipine is a calcium channel blocker of the dihydropyridine class. It sold in the United States under the proprietary name Sular. Nisoldipine has tropism for cardiac blood vessels.
Calcium channel blocker	A calcium channel blocker is a chemical that disrupts the movement of calcium (Ca^{2+}) through calcium channels. Calcium channel blockers drugs devised to target neurons are used as antiepileptics. However, the most widespread clinical usage of calcium channel blockers is to decrease blood pressure in patients with hypertension.
Benazepril	Benazepril, brand name Lotensin, is a medication used to treat high blood pressure (hypertension), congestive heart failure, and chronic renal failure. Upon cleavage of its ester group by the liver, benazepril is converted into its active form benazeprilat, a non-sulfhydryl angiotensin-converting enzyme (ACE) inhibitor.
Captopril	Captopril (rINN) is an angiotensin-converting enzyme (ACE) inhibitor used for the treatment of hypertension and some types of congestive heart failure. Captopril was the first ACE inhibitor developed and was considered a breakthrough both because of its novel mechanism of action and also because of the revolutionary development process. Captopril is commonly marketed by Bristol-Myers Squibb under the trade name Capoten.
Eprosartan	Eprosartan is an angiotensin II receptor antagonist used for the treatment of high blood pressure.

	It is marketed as Teveten by Abbott Laboratories in the United States. It is marketed as Eprozar by INTAS Pharmaceuticals in India and by Abbott Laboratories elsewhere. It is sometimes paired with hydrochlorothiazide, marketed in the US as Teveten HCT and elsewhere as Teveten Plus.
Fosinopril	Fosinopril is an angiotensin converting enzyme (ACE) inhibitor used for the treatment of hypertension and some types of chronic heart failure. Fosinopril is the only phosphinate-containing ACE inhibitor marketed. It is marketed by Bristol-Myers Squibb under the trade name Monopril.
Lisinopril	Lisinopril is a drug of the angiotensin-converting enzyme (ACE) inhibitor class that is primarily used in treatment of hypertension, congestive heart failure, and heart attacks and also in preventing renal and retinal complications of diabetes. Its indications, contraindications and side effects are as those for all ACE inhibitors. It has been compared with omapatrilat, which is of similar function.
Moexipril hydrochloride	Moexipril hydrochloride is a potent orally active non-sulfhydryl angiotensin converting enzyme inhibitor (ACE) which is used for the treatment of hypertension and congestive heart failure. Moexipril can be administered alone or together with other antihypertensives or diuretics. It works by inhibiting the conversion of angiotensin I to angiotensin II. Moexipril is available from Schwarz'Pharma under the trade name Univasc.
Perindopril	Perindopril, (trade names include Coversyl and Aceon) is a long-acting ACE inhibitor. Perindopril is used to treat high blood pressure, heart failure or stable coronary artery disease. It is also available in a generic form, perindopril erbumine.
Ramipril	Ramipril is an angiotensin-converting enzyme inhibitor, used to treat high blood pressure and congestive heart failure. It is marketed as Prilace by Arrow Pharmaceuticals in Australia, Ramipro by Westfield Pharma in the Philippines, Tritace by Sanofi-Aventis in Italy and United States and Altace by King Pharmaceuticals in the United States, Ramitens by PharmaSwiss, Ampril by Krka in Slovenia, Corpril by Cemelog-BRS in Hungary, Piramil and Prilinda by Hemofarm in Serbia, by Lek in Poland and by Novartis in Bangladesh, and in Canada as Altace (Sonfi) and Ramipril.
Valsartan	Valsartan (Angiotan or Diovan) is an angiotensin II receptor antagonist (more commonly called an 'ARB', or angiotensin receptor blocker), with particularly high affinity for the type I (AT_1) angiotensin receptor. By blocking the action of angiotensin, valsartan dilates blood vessels and reduces blood pressure. In the U.S., valsartan is indicated for treatment of high blood pressure, congestive heart failure (CHF), or post-myocardial infarction (MI).
Quinapril	Quinapril is an angiotensin-converting enzyme inhibitor (ACE inhibitor) used in the treatment of hypertension and congestive heart failure.
Renal failure	Renal failure is a medical condition in which the kidneys fail to adequately filter waste products from the blood. The two main forms are acute kidney injury, which is often reversible with adequate treatment, and chronic kidney disease, which is often not reversible.

6. UNIT-6 Cardiovascular Agents,

Angioedema	Angioedema or Quincke's edema is the rapid swelling (edema) of the dermis, subcutaneous tissue, mucosa and submucosal tissues. It is very similar to urticaria, but urticaria, commonly known as hives, occurs in the upper dermis. The term angioneurotic oedema was used for this condition in the belief that there was nervous system involvement, but this is no longer thought to be the case.
Adenosine	Adenosine is a purine nucleoside composed of a molecule of adenine attached to a ribose sugar molecule (ribofuranose) moiety via a ß-N_9-glycosidic bond. Adenosine plays an important role in biochemical processes, such as energy transfer -- as adenosine triphosphate (ATP) and adenosine diphosphate (ADP) -- as well as in signal transduction as cyclic adenosine monophosphate (cAMP). It is also a neuromodulator, believed to play a role in promoting sleep and suppressing arousal.
Dofetilide	Dofetilide is a class III antiarrhythmic agent. It is marketed under the trade name Tikosyn by Pfizer, and is available in the United States in capsules containing 125, 250, and 500 µg of dofetilide. Due to the pro-arrhythmic potential of dofetilide, it is only available by prescription by physicians who have undergone specific training in the risks of treatment with dofetilide.
Dronedarone	Dronedarone is a drug by Sanofi-Aventis, mainly for the indication of cardiac arrhythmias. It was approved by the FDA on July 2, 2009. It was recommended as an alternative to amiodarone for the treatment of atrial fibrillation and atrial flutter in people whose hearts have either returned to normal rhythm or who undergo drug therapy or electric shock treatment i.e. direct current cardioversion (DCCV) to maintain normal rhythm. However, the FDA did not approve dronedarone for reducing deaths.
Flecainide	Flecainide acetate is a class Ic antiarrhythmic agent used to prevent and treat tachyarrhythmias (abnormal fast rhythms of the heart). It is used to treat a variety of cardiac arrhythmias including paroxysmal atrial fibrillation (episodic irregular heartbeat originating in the upper chamber of the heart), paroxysmal supraventricular tachycardia (episodic rapid but regular heartbeat originating in the atrium), and ventricular tachycardia (rapid rhythms of the lower chambers of the heart). Flecainide works by regulating the flow of sodium in the heart, causing prolongation of the cardiac action potential.
Ibutilide	Ibutilide is a Class III antiarrhythmic agent that is indicated for acute cardioconversion of atrial fibrillation and atrial flutter of a recent onset to sinus rhythm. It exerts its antiarrhythmic effect by induction of slow inward sodium current, which prolongs action potential and refractory period (physiology) of myocardial cells. Because of its Class III antiarrhythmic activity, there should not be concomitant administration of Class Ia and Class III agents.

Mexiletine	Mexiletine belongs to the Class IB anti-arrhythmic group of medicines. It is used to treat arrhythmias within the heart, or seriously irregular heartbeats. It slows conduction in the heart and makes the heart tissue less sensitive.
Procainamide	Procainamide INN is a pharmaceutical antiarrhythmic agent used for the medical treatment of cardiac arrhythmias, classified by the Vaughan Williams classification system as class Ia.
Quinidine	Quinidine is a pharmaceutical agent that acts as a class I antiarrhythmic agent in the heart. It is a stereoisomer of quinine, originally derived from the bark of the cinchona tree. The drug causes increased action potential duration, as well as a prolonged QT interval.
Tachycardia	Tachycardia is a heart rate that exceeds the normal range. In general, a resting heart rate over 100 beats per minute is accepted as tachycardia. Tachycardia can be caused by various factors that often are benign.
Tocainide	Tocainide is a class Ib antiarrhythmic agent. It is no longer sold in the United States.
	Quick look at the Pharmacokinetics
	Tocainide is a lidocaine analog, that does not have significant 1st pass metabolism.
Antiarrhythmic agent	Antiarrhythmic agents are a group of pharmaceuticals that are used to suppress abnormal rhythms of the heart, such as atrial fibrillation, atrial flutter, ventricular tachycardia, and ventricular fibrillation.
	Many attempts have been made to classify antiarrhythmic agents. The problem arises from the fact that many of the antiarrhythmic agents have multiple modes of action, making any classification imprecise.
Disopyramide	Disopyramide (INN, trade names Norpace and Rythmodan) is an antiarrhythmic medication used in the treatment of Ventricular Tachycardia. It is a sodium channel blocker and therefore classified as a Class 1a anti-arrhythmic agent.' Disopyramide has a negative inotropic effect on the ventricular myocardium, significantly decreasing the contractility.' Disopyramide also has an anticholinergic effect on the heart which accounts for many adverse side effects. Disopyramide is available in both oral and intravenous forms, and has a low degree of toxicity.
Cholestyramine	Cholestyramine or colestyramine is a bile acid sequestrant, which binds bile in the gastrointestinal tract to prevent its reabsorption. It is a strong ion exchange resin, which means that it can exchange its chloride anions with anionic bile acids in the gastrointestinal tract and bind them strongly in the resin matrix. The functional group of the anion exchange resin is a quaternary ammonium group attached to an inert styrene-divinylbenzene copolymer.
Ezetimibe	Ezetimibe is a drug that lowers plasma cholesterol levels.

	It acts by decreasing cholesterol absorption in the intestine. It may be used alone (marketed as Zetia or Ezetrol), when other cholesterol-lowering medications are not tolerated, or together with statins (e.g., ezetimibe/simvastatin, marketed as Vytorin and Inegy) when statins alone do not control cholesterol.
Fenofibrate	Fenofibrate is a drug of the fibrate class. Fenofibrate was developed by Groupe Fournier SA, before it was acquired in 2005 by Solvay Pharmaceutical, a business unit owned by the Belgian corporation, Solvay S.A. In 2009 Solvay Pharmaceutical was acquired by Abbott Laboratories. It is mainly used to reduce cholesterol levels in patients at risk of cardiovascular disease.
Gemfibrozil	Gemfibrozil is the generic name for an oral drug used to lower lipid levels. It belongs to a group of drugs known as fibrates. It is most commonly sold as the brand name, Lopid. Other brand names include Jezil and Gen-Fibro.
Hyperlipidemia	Hyperlipidemia, hyperlipoproteinemia, or hyperlipidaemia involves abnormally elevated levels of any or all lipids and/or lipoproteins in the blood. It is the most common form of dyslipidemia (which also includes any decreased lipid levels). Lipids (fat-soluble molecules) are transported in a protein capsule.
Niacin	Niacin is an organic compound with the formula $C_6H_5NO_2$ and, depending on the definition used, one of the 40 to 80 essential human nutrients. Niacin is one of five vitamins (when lacking in human diet) associated with a pandemic deficiency disease: niacin deficiency (pellagra), vitamin C deficiency (scurvy), thiamin deficiency (beriberi), vitamin D deficiency (rickets and osteomalacia), vitamin A deficiency (night blindness and other symptoms). Niacin has been used for over 50 years to increase levels of HDL in the blood and has been found to decrease the risk of cardiovascular events modestly in a number of controlled human trials.
Nicotinic acid	Niacin (also known as vitamin B_3, nicotinic acid, or less commonly vitamin PP; archaic terms include pellagra-preventive and anti-dermatitis factor) is an organic compound with the formula $C_6H_5NO_2$ and, depending on the definition used, one of the 40 to 80 essential human nutrients. Niacin is one of five vitamins associated with a pandemic deficiency disease: niacin deficiency (pellagra), vitamin C deficiency (scurvy), thiamin deficiency (beriberi), vitamin D deficiency (rickets and osteomalacia), vitamin A deficiency (night blindness and other symptoms). Niacin has been used for over 50 years to increase levels of HDL in the blood and has been found to decrease the risk of cardiovascular events modestly in a number of controlled human trials.
Pitavastatin	Pitavastatin is a member of the medication class of statins, marketed in the United States under the trade name Livalo.

	Like other statins, it is an inhibitor of HMG-CoA reductase, the enzyme that catalyses the first step of cholesterol synthesis. It has been available in Japan since 2003, and is being marketed under licence in South Korea and in India.
Pravastatin	Pravastatin is a member of the drug class of statins, used in combination with diet, exercise, and weight-loss for lowering cholesterol and preventing cardiovascular disease.
Simvastatin	Simvastatin ( ) is a hypolipidemic drug used to control elevated cholesterol, or hypercholesterolemia. It is a member of the statin class of pharmaceuticals.
	Simvastatin is a synthetic derivate of a fermentation product of Aspergillus terreus.
Colestipol	Colestipol is a bile acid sequestrant used to lower blood cholesterol, specifically low-density lipoprotein (LDL).
	Like cholestyramine, colestipol works in the gut by trapping bile acids and preventing them from being reabsorbed. This leads to decreased enterohepatic recirculation of bile acids, increased synthesis of new bile acids by the liver from cholesterol, decreased liver cholesterol, increased LDL receptor expression, and decreasing LDL in blood.
Red yeast rice	Red yeast rice ; pinyin: hóng qu mi; literally 'red yeast rice'), red rice koji (?????, lit. 'red koji') or akakoji (????, also meaning 'red koji'), red fermented rice, red kojic rice, red koji rice, anka, or ang-kak (Hokkien Chinese borrowed from Tagalog), is a bright reddish purple fermented rice, which acquires its colour from being cultivated with the mold Monascus purpureus.
	Red yeast rice is what is referred to, in Japanese, as a koji, meaning 'grain or bean overgrown with a mold culture', a food preparation tradition going back to ca. 300 BC. In both the scientific and popular literature in English that draws principally on Japanese, it is most often known as 'red rice koji'.
Abciximab	Abciximab a glycoprotein IIb/IIIa receptor antagonist manufactured by Janssen Biologics BV and distributed by Eli Lilly under the trade name ReoPro, is a platelet aggregation inhibitor mainly used during and after coronary artery procedures like angioplasty to prevent platelets from sticking together and causing thrombus (blood clot) formation within the coronary artery. It is a glycoprotein IIb/IIIa inhibitor.
	While Abciximab has a short plasma half-life, due to its strong affinity for its receptor on the platelets, it may occupy some receptors for weeks.
Anisindione	Anisindione is a synthetic anticoagulant and an indanedione derivative.

6. UNIT-6 Cardiovascular Agents,

Aspirin	Aspirin also known as acetylsalicylic acid , is a salicylate drug, often used as an analgesic to relieve minor aches and pains, as an antipyretic to reduce fever, and as an anti-inflammatory medication. Aspirin was first isolated by Felix Hoffmann, a chemist with the German company Bayer in 1897. Salicylic acid, the main metabolite of aspirin, is an integral part of human and animal metabolism.
Clopidogrel	Clopidogrel is an oral, thienopyridine class antiplatelet agent used to inhibit blood clots in coronary artery disease, peripheral vascular disease, and cerebrovascular disease. It is marketed by Bristol-Myers Squibb and Sanofi-Aventis under the trade name Plavix. The drug works by irreversibly inhibiting a receptor called $P2Y_{12}$, an adenosine diphosphate ADP chemoreceptor.
Dalteparin	Dalteparin is a low molecular weight heparin. It is marketed as Fragmin by Pfizer Inc. Like other low molecular weight heparins, dalteparin is used for prophylaxis or treatment of deep vein thrombosis and pulmonary embolism.
Fondaparinux	Fondaparinux is an anticoagulant medication chemically related to low molecular weight heparins. It is marketed by GlaxoSmithKline. A generic version developed by Alchemia is marketed within the US by Dr. Reddy's Laboratories.
Streptokinase	Staphylokinase/Streptokinase family Streptokinase a protein secreted by several species of streptococci can bind and activate human plasminogen. SK is used as an effective and inexpensive thrombolysis medication in some cases of myocardial infarction (heart attack) and pulmonary embolism. Streptokinase belongs to a group of medications known as fibrinolytics, and complexes of streptokinase with human plasminogen can hydrolytically activate other unbound plasminogen by activating through bond cleavage to produce plasmin.
Ticlopidine	Ticlopidine (trade name Ticlid) is an antiplatelet drug in the thienopyridine family. Like clopidogrel, it is an adenosine diphosphate (ADP) receptor inhibitor. It is used in patients in whom aspirin is not tolerated, or in whom dual antiplatelet therapy is desirable.
Tinzaparin	Tinzaparin is an antithrombotic drug in the heparin group. It is a low molecular weight heparin (LMWH) marketed as Innohep worldwide. It has been approved by the U.S. Food and Drug Administration (FDA) for once daily treatment and prophylaxis of deep vein thrombosis and pulmonary embolism.
Warfarin	Warfarin is an anticoagulant. It is most likely to be the drug popularly referred to as a 'blood thinner,' yet this is a misnomer, since it does not affect the thickness or viscosity of blood.

Low molecular weight heparin	In medicine, low-molecular-weight heparin is a class of medication used as an anticoagulant in diseases that feature thrombosis, as well as for prophylaxis in situations that lead to a high risk of thrombosis.
	Thrombotic disease or thrombosis is the formation of a clot within a blood vessel which interferes with the blood supply to tissues and causes problems such as deep vein thrombosis, pulmonary embolism when it is located in the veins, or heart attacks and strokes when located in the arteries.
	Heparin is a naturally occurring polysaccharide that inhibits coagulation, the process whereby thrombosis occurs . Natural heparin consists of molecular chains of varying lengths, or molecular weights. Chains of molecular weight from 5000 to over 40,000 Daltons, making up polydisperse pharmaceutical-grade heparin.
	Heparin derived from natural sources, mainly porcine intestine or bovine lung, can be administered therapeutically to prevent thrombosis. However, the effects of natural, or unfractionated heparin can be difficult to predict. After a standard dose of unfractionated heparin, coagulation parameters must be monitored very closely to prevent over- or under-anticoagulation.
	Low-molecular-weight heparins , in contrast, consist of only short chains of polysaccharide. low\ molecular\ weight\ heparins are defined as heparin salts having an average molecular weight of less than 8000 Da and for which at least 60% of all chains have a molecular weight less than 8000 Da. These are obtained by various methods of fractionation or depolymerisation of polymeric heparin. Anti-factor Xa activity
	Coagulation cascade is a normal physiological process which aims at preventing significant blood loss or hemorrhage following vascular injury. Unfortunately, there are times when a blood clot (thrombus) will form when it is not needed. For instance, some high risk conditions such as acute medical illness prolonged immobilization, surgery, or cancer can increase the risk of developing a blood clot which can potentially lead to significant consequences.
	The coagulation cascade consists of a series of steps in which a protease cleaves and subsequently activates the next protease in the sequence. Since each protease can activate several molecules of the next protease in the series, this biological cascade is amplified. The final result of these reactions is to convert fibrinogen, a soluble protein, to insoluble threads of fibrin. Together with platelets, the fibrin threads form a stable blood clot.
	Antithrombin (AT), a serine protease inhibitor, is the major plasma inhibitor of coagulation proteases. low\ molecular\ weight\ heparins inhibit the coagulation process through binding to AT via a pentasaccharide sequence. This binding leads to a conformational change of AT which accelerates its inhibition of thrombin (factor IIa) and activated factor X (factor Xa). Once dissociated, the low\ molecular\ weight\ heparin is free to bind to another antithrombin molecule and subsequently inhibit more thrombin.

6. UNIT-6 Cardiovascular Agents,

The effects of low\ molecular\ weight\ heparins cannot be acceptably measured using the partial thromboplastin time (PTT) or activated clotting time (ACT) tests. Rather, low\ molecular\ weight\ heparin therapy is monitored by the anti-factor Xa assay, measuring anti-factor Xa activity. The methodology of an anti-factor Xa assay is that patient plasma is added to a known amount of excess factor Xa and excess antithrombin. If heparin or low\ molecular\ weight\ heparin is present in the patient plasma, it will bind to antithrombin and form a complex with factor Xa, inhibiting it. The amount of residual factor Xa is inversely proportional to the amount of heparin/low\ molecular\ weight\ heparin in the plasma. The amount of residual factor Xa is detected by adding a chromogenic substrate that mimics the natural substrate of factor Xa, making residual factor Xa cleave it, releasing a colored compound that can be detected by a spectrophotometer. Antithrombin deficiencies in the patient do not affect the assay, because excess amounts of antithrombin is provided in the reaction. Results are given in anticoagulant concentration in units/mL of antifactor Xa, such that high values indicate high levels of anticoagulation and low values indicate low levels of anticoagulation.

low\ molecular\ weight\ heparins have a potency of greater than 70 units/mg of anti-factor Xa activity and a ratio of anti-factor Xa activity to anti-thrombin activity of >1.5.

Table 1 Molecular weight (MW) data and anticoagulant activities of currently available low\ molecular\ weight\ heparin products. Adapted from Gray E et al. 2008. Manufacturing Process

Various methods of heparin depolymerisation are used in the manufacture of low-molecular-weight heparin. These are listed below:•Oxidative depolymerisation with hydrogen peroxide. Used in the manufacture of ardeparin (Normiflo)•Deaminative cleavage with isoamyl nitrite. Used in the manufacture of certoparin (Sandoparin)•Alkaline beta-eliminative cleavage of the benzyl ester of heparin. Used in the manufacture of enoxaparin (Lovenox and Clexane)•Oxidative depolymerisation with Cu^{2+} and hydrogen peroxide. Used in the manufacture of parnaparin (Fluxum)•Beta-eliminative cleavage by the heparinase enzyme. Used in the manufacture of tinzaparin (Innohep and Logiparin)•Deaminative cleavage with nitrous acid. Used in the manufacture of dalteparin (Fragmin), reviparin (Clivarin) and nadroparin (Fraxiparin)

Deaminative cleavage with nitrous acid results in the formation of an unnatural anhydromannose residue at the reducing terminal of the oligosaccharides produced. This can subsequently be converted to anhydromannitol using a suitable reducing agent as shown in figure 1.

Likewise both chemical and enzymatic beta-elimination result in the formation of an unnatural unsaturated uronate residue(UA) at the non-reducing terminal. Differences between low molecular weight heparin products

Comparisons between low\ molecular\ weight\ heparins prepared by similar processes vary.

6. UNIT-6 Cardiovascular Agents,

Dabigatran	Dabigatran is an oral anticoagulant from the class of the direct thrombin inhibitors. It is used for various clinical indications, and in some cases it offers an alternative to warfarin as the preferred orally administered anticoagulant ('blood thinner'), since it does not require frequent blood tests for international normalized ratio monitoring, while offering similar results in terms of efficacy. No specific way exists to reverse the anticoagulant effect of dabigatran in the event of a major bleeding event, unlike warfarin.
Prasugrel	Prasugrel is a platelet inhibitor developed by Daiichi Sankyo Co. and produced by Ube and currently marketed in the United States in cooperation with Eli Lilly and Company for acute coronary syndromes planned for percutaneous coronary intervention (PCI). Prasugrel was approved for use in Europe in February 2009, and is currently available in the UK. On July 10, 2009, the US Food and Drug Administration approved the use of prasugrel for the reduction of thrombotic cardiovascular events (including stent thrombosis) in patients with acute coronary syndrome who are to be managed with PCI.
Pulmonary embolism	Pulmonary embolism is a blockage of the main artery of the lung or one of its branches by a substance that has travelled from elsewhere in the body through the bloodstream (embolism). PE most commonly results from deep vein thrombosis (a blood clot in the deep veins of the legs or pelvis) that breaks off and migrates to the lung, a process termed venous thromboembolism (VTE). A small proportion of cases are caused by the embolization of air, fat, or talc in drugs of intravenous drug abusers or amniotic fluid.
Vitamin K	Vitamin K is a group of structurally similar, fat-soluble vitamins that are needed for the posttranslational modification of certain proteins required for blood coagulation and in metabolic pathways in bone and other tissue. They are 2-methyl-1,4-naphthoquinone (3-) derivatives. This group of vitamins includes two natural vitamers: vitamin K_1 and vitamin K_2.
Heparin	Heparin (from Ancient Greek ηπαρ (hepar), liver), also known as unfractionated heparin, a highly sulfated glycosaminoglycan, is widely used as an injectable anticoagulant, and has the highest negative charge density of any known biological molecule. It can also be used to form an inner anticoagulant surface on various experimental and medical devices such as test tubes and renal dialysis machines. Although it is used principally in medicine for anticoagulation, its true physiological role in the body remains unclear, because blood anti-coagulation is achieved mostly by heparan sulfate proteoglycans derived from endothelial cells.
Stroke	A stroke, is the rapid loss of brain function due to disturbance in the blood supply to the brain. This can be due to ischemia (lack of blood flow) caused by blockage (thrombosis, arterial embolism), or a hemorrhage.

6. UNIT-6 Cardiovascular Agents,

Phosphodiesterase inhibitor	A phosphodiesterase inhibitor is a drug that blocks one or more of the five subtypes of the enzyme phosphodiesterase, thereby preventing the inactivation of the intracellular second messengers cyclic adenosine monophosphate (cAMP) and cyclic guanosine monophosphate (cGMP) by the respective PDE subtype(s).
Anticoagulant	An anticoagulant is a substance that prevents coagulation (clotting) of blood. Such substances occur naturally in leeches and blood-sucking insects. A group of pharmaceuticals called anticoagulants can be used in vivo as a medication for thrombotic disorders.
Cilostazol	Cilostazol is a medication used in the alleviation of the symptom of intermittent claudication in individuals with peripheral vascular disease. It is manufactured by Otsuka Pharmaceutical Co. under the trade name Pletal.
Enoxaparin	Enoxaparin is a low molecular weight heparin marketed under the trade names Lovenox, Xaparin and Clexane, among others. It is an anticoagulant used to prevent and treat deep vein thrombosis or pulmonary embolism, and is given as a subcutaneous injection (by a health care provider or the patient). Its use is evolving in acute coronary syndromes (ACS).

1. _____, trade names Minipress, Vasoflex, Pressin and Hypovase, is a sympatholytic drug used to treat high blood pressure and anxiety, PTSD, and panic disorder. It is an alpha-adrenergic blocker that is specific for the alpha-1 receptors. These receptors are found on vascular smooth muscle, where they are responsible for the vasoconstrictive action of norepinephrine.

    a. Tigan
    b. Tirofiban
    c. Trimethobenzamide
    d. Prazosin

2. . _____ (as besylate, mesylate or maleate) is a long-acting calcium channel blocker dihydropyridine (DHP) class used as an antihypertensive and in the treatment of angina pectoris. Like other calcium channel blockers, _____ acts by relaxing the smooth muscle in the arterial wall, decreasing total peripheral resistance thereby reducing blood pressure; in angina, _____ increases blood flow to the heart muscle (although DHP-class calcium channel blockers are more selective for arteries than the muscular tissue of the heart (myocardium), as the cardiac calcium channels are not of the dihydropyridine-type).

    a. Arecoline

b. Articaine

c. Enprostil

d. Amlodipine

3. A _____ is a chemical that disrupts the movement of calcium (Ca^{2+}) through calcium channels.

_____s drugs devised to target neurons are used as antiepileptics. However, the most widespread clinical usage of _____s is to decrease blood pressure in patients with hypertension.

a. Homeopathic

b. Pranidipine

c. Calcium channel blocker

d. TROX-1

4. _____ is a drug of the angiotensin-converting enzyme (ACE) inhibitor class that is primarily used in treatment of hypertension, congestive heart failure, and heart attacks and also in preventing renal and retinal complications of diabetes. Its indications, contraindications and side effects are as those for all ACE inhibitors. It has been compared with omapatrilat, which is of similar function.

a. Mecillinam

b. Lisinopril

c. Mezlocillin

d. Penicillamine

5. _____ (trade names Tekturna, US; Rasilez, UK and elsewhere) is the first in a class of drugs called direct renin inhibitors. Its current licensed indication is essential (primary) hypertension.

_____ was co-developed by the Swiss pharmaceutical companies Novartis and Speedel.

a. Atenolol

b. Avandia

c. Adapalene

d. Aliskiren

1. d
2. d
3. c
4. b
5. d

You can take the complete Online Interactive Chapter Practice Test

for 6. UNIT-6 Cardiovascular Agents,
on all key terms, persons, places, and concepts.

No Additional Costs

http://www.Cram101.com

Register, send an email request to Travis.Reese@Cram101.com to get your user Id and password.

Include your customer order number, and ISBN number from your studyguide Retailer.

7. UNIT-7 Gastrointestinal Agents,

CHAPTER OUTLINE: KEY TERMS, PEOPLE, PLACES, CONCEPTS

- Antacid
- Gastroesophageal reflux disease
- Magnesium oxide
- Mechanism of action
- Cimetidine
- Esomeprazole
- Lansoprazole
- Nizatidine
- Pantoprazole
- Rabeprazole
- Peptic ulcer disease
- Peptic
- Secretion
- Helicobacter pylori
- Pharmacokinetics
- Bisacodyl
- Dioctyl sodium sulfosuccinate
- Laxatives
- Magnesium citrate
- Methylcellulose
- Mineral oil

CHAPTER OUTLINE: KEY TERMS, PEOPLE, PLACES, CONCEPTS

	Polyethylene glycol
	Psyllium
	Sodium phosphate
	Sorbitol
	Irritable bowel syndrome
	Enema
	Magnesium sulfate
	Paregoric
	Clostridium difficile
	Rehydration
	Anticholinergic
	Aprepitant
	Dolasetron
	Metoclopramide
	Ondansetron
	Scopolamine
	Antiemetic
	Receptor antagonist
	Postoperative nausea and vomiting
	Alosetron
	Misoprostol

	Simethicone
	Sucralfate
	Ursodiol

Antacid	An antacid is a substance which neutralizes stomach acidity.
Gastroesophageal reflux disease	Gastroesophageal reflux disease, gastro-oesophageal reflux disease (GORD), gastric reflux disease, or acid reflux disease is a chronic symptom of mucosal damage caused by stomach acid coming up from the stomach into the esophagus. GERD is usually caused by changes in the barrier between the stomach and the esophagus, including abnormal relaxation of the lower esophageal sphincter, which normally holds the top of the stomach closed, impaired expulsion of gastric reflux from the esophagus, or a hiatal hernia. These changes may be permanent or temporary.
Magnesium oxide	Magnesium oxide or magnesia, is a white hygroscopic solid mineral that occurs naturally as periclase and is a source of magnesium . It has an empirical formula of MgO and consists of a lattice of Mg^{2+} ions and O^{2-} ions held together by ionic bonds. Magnesium hydroxide forms in the presence of water ($MgO + H_2O \rightarrow Mg(OH)_2$), but it can be reversed by heating it to separate moisture.
Mechanism of action	In pharmacology, the term mechanism of action refers to the specific biochemical interaction through which a drug substance produces its pharmacological effect. A mechanism of action usually includes mention of the specific molecular targets to which the drug binds, such as an enzyme or receptor. For example, the mechanism of action of aspirin involves irreversible inhibition of the enzyme cyclooxygenase, therefore suppressing the production of prostaglandins and thromboxanes, thereby reducing pain and inflammation.
Cimetidine	Cimetidine INN is a histamine H_2-receptor antagonist that inhibits stomach acid production. It is largely used in the treatment of heartburn and peptic ulcers.

CHAPTER HIGHLIGHTS & NOTES: KEY TERMS, PEOPLE, PLACES, CONCEPTS

Esomeprazole	Esomeprazole is a proton pump inhibitor (brand name Nexium) which reduces acid secretion through inhibition of the H+ / K+ ATPase in gastric parietal cells. By inhibiting the functioning of this transporter, the drug prevents formation of gastric acid. It is used in the treatment of dyspepsia, peptic ulcer disease (PUD), gastroesophageal reflux disease (GORD/GERD) and Zollinger-Ellison syndrome.
Lansoprazole	Lansoprazole is a proton-pump inhibitor (PPI) which inhibits the stomach's production of gastric acids. It is manufactured by a number of companies worldwide under several brand names. In the United States it was first approved by the Food and Drug Administration (FDA) in 1995.
Nizatidine	Nizatidine is a histamine H_2-receptor antagonist that inhibits stomach acid production, and commonly used in the treatment of peptic ulcer disease and gastroesophageal reflux disease (GERD). It was developed by Eli Lilly and is marketed under the brand names Tazac and Axid.
Pantoprazole	Pantoprazole is a proton pump inhibitor drug that inhibits gastric acid secretion.
Rabeprazole	Rabeprazole is an antiulcer drug in the class of proton pump inhibitors. It was developed by Eisai Co. and is marketed by Janssen-Cilag as rabeprazole sodium under the brand names AcipHex in the US and Pariet in Britain, Italy, Greece, Australia, Brazil, Canada, Japan, and Russia.
Peptic ulcer disease	A peptic ulcer, also known as peptic ulcer disease is the most common ulcer of an area of the gastrointestinal tract that is usually acidic and thus extremely painful. It is defined as mucosal erosions equal to or greater than 0.5 cm. As many as 70-90% of such ulcers are associated with Helicobacter pylori, a helical-shaped bacterium that lives in the acidic environment of the stomach; however, only 40% of those cases go to a doctor.
Peptic	Peptic is an adjective that refers to any part of the body that normally has an acidic lumen. 'Peptic' is medical and veterinary terminology, most often used in the context of humans.
Secretion	Secretion is the process of elaborating, releasing, and oozing chemicals, or a secreted chemical substance from a cell or gland. In contrast to excretion, the substance may have a certain function, rather than being a waste product. Many cells contain this such as glucoma cells.
Helicobacter pylori	Helicobacter pylori previously named Campylobacter pyloridis, is a Gram-negative, microaerophilic bacterium found in the stomach. It was identified in 1982 by Barry Marshall and Robin Warren, who found that it was present in patients with chronic gastritis and gastric ulcers, conditions that were not previously believed to have a microbial cause. It is also linked to the development of duodenal ulcers and stomach cancer.
Pharmacokinetics	Pharmacokinetics, is a branch of pharmacology dedicated to the determination of the fate of substances administered externally to a living organism.

7. UNIT-7 Gastrointestinal Agents,

	The substances of interest include pharmaceutical agents, hormones, nutrients, and toxins.
	Pharmacokinetics includes the study of the mechanisms of absorption and distribution of an administered drug, the chemical changes of the substance in the body (e.g. by metabolic enzymes such as CYP or UGT enzymes), and the effects and routes of excretion of the metabolites of the drug.
Bisacodyl	Bisacodyl is a stimulant laxative drug that works directly on the colon to produce a bowel movement. It is typically prescribed for relief of constipation and for the management of neurogenic bowel dysfunction as well as part of bowel preparation before medical examinations, such as for a colonoscopy. Bisacodyl is a diphenylmethane (in fact, a modified triphenylmethane) derivative and was first used as a laxative in 1953 due to its similarity to phenolphthalein.
Dioctyl sodium sulfosuccinate	Dioctyl sodium sulfosuccinate or docusate sodium -, especially laxatives of the stool softener type. It is also used as an emulsifying, wetting, and dispersing agent, as a pesticide, as well as a component of the oil dispersant Corexit which was used in the Deepwater Horizon oil spill of 2010. It is an anionic surfactant, a substance that lowers the surface tension of water. Docusate calcium and docusate potassium, as well as other dioctyl sulfosuccinate salts, are also widely used in the same areas.
Laxatives	Laxatives are foods, compounds or drugs taken to loosen the stool, most often taken to treat constipation. Certain stimulant, lubricant and saline laxatives are used to evacuate the colon for rectal and/or bowel examinations, and may be supplemented by enemas under certain circumstances. Sufficiently high doses of laxatives may cause diarrhea.
Magnesium citrate	Magnesium citrate, a magnesium preparation in salt form with citric acid, is a chemical agent used medicinally as a saline laxative and to completely empty the bowel prior to a major surgery or colonoscopy. It is available without a prescription, both as a generic or under the brand name Citromag or Citroma. It is also used in pill form as a magnesium dietary supplement.
Methylcellulose	Methyl cellulose (or methylcellulose) is a chemical compound derived from cellulose. It is a hydrophilic white powder in pure form and dissolves in cold (but not in hot) water, forming a clear viscous solution or gel. It is sold under a variety of trade names and is used as a thickener and emulsifier in various food and cosmetic products, and also as a treatment of constipation.
Mineral oil	A mineral oil is any of various colorless, odorless, light mixtures of alkanes in the C15 to C40 range from a non-vegetable (mineral) source, particularly a distillate of petroleum. The name mineral oil by itself is imprecise, having been used to label many specific oils over the past few centuries.

Polyethylene glycol	Polyethylene glycol is a polyether compound with many applications from industrial manufacturing to medicine. The structure of PEG is (note the repeated element in parentheses):$H\text{-}(O\text{-}CH_2\text{-}CH_2)_n\text{-}OH$
	PEG is also known as polyethylene oxide (PEO) or polyoxyethylene (POE), depending on its molecular weight.
Psyllium	Psyllium, or Ispaghula, is the common name used for several members of the plant genus Plantago whose seeds are used commercially for the production of mucilage.
Sodium phosphate	Sodium phosphate is a generic term for the salts of sodium hydroxide and phosphoric acid. They are:•sodium dihydrogen phosphate, commonly termed monosodium phosphate, (NaH_2PO_4), is also known as 'sodium phosphate, monobasic'•disodium hydrogen phosphate, commonly termed disodium phosphate, (Na_2HPO_4) is also known as 'sodium phosphate, dibasic'•Trisodium phosphate, commonly shortened to just sodium phosphate, (Na_3PO_4), is also known as 'sodium phosphate, tribasic'•sodium aluminium phosphate, $(Na_8Al_2(OH)_2(PO_4)_4)$
	Sodium phosphates are often used as meat preservatives, as an alternative to sodium nitrite. This is common in canned meats.
Sorbitol	Sorbitol, is a sugar alcohol that the human body metabolizes slowly. It can be obtained by reduction of glucose, changing the aldehyde group to a hydroxyl group. Sorbitol is found in apples, pears, peaches, and prunes.
Irritable bowel syndrome	Irritable bowel syndrome is a symptom-based diagnosis characterized by chronic abdominal pain, discomfort, bloating, and alteration of bowel habits. As a functional gastrointestinal disorder (FGID), irritable bowel syndrome has no known organic cause. Diarrhea or constipation may predominate, or they may alternate (classified as irritable bowel syndrome-D, irritable bowel syndrome-C, or irritable bowel syndrome-A, respectively).
Enema	An enema or clyster, is a fluid injected into the lower bowel by way of the rectum.
	The most frequent use of an enema is as or cleansing enema which is given to relieve constipation or for bowel cleansing before a medical examination or procedure.
	In standard medicine an enema may also be employed as a lower gastrointestinal series (also called a barium enema), to check diarrhea, as a vehicle for the administration of food, water or medicine, as a stimulant to the general system, as a local application and, more rarely, as a means of reducing temperature as treatment for encopresis, and as rehydration therapy in patients for whom intravenous therapy is not applicable.

7. UNIT-7 Gastrointestinal Agents,

Magnesium sulfate	Magnesium sulfate is a chemical compound containing magnesium, sulfur and oxygen, with the formula $MgSO_4$. It is often encountered as the heptahydrate epsomite ($MgSO_4 \cdot 7H_2O$), commonly called Epsom salt, from the town of Epsom in Surrey, England, where the salt was distilled from the springs that arise where the porous chalk of the North Downs meets non-porous London clay. Another hydrate form is kieserite.
Paregoric	Paregoric, also known as tinctura opii camphorata, is a medication known for its antidiarrheal, antitussive, and analgesic properties. In the early 18th century Jakob Le Mort (1650-1718), a professor of chemistry at Leiden University, prepared an elixir for asthma and called it 'paregoric'. The word 'paregoric' comes from the Greek word 'paregoricon' which was originally applied to oratory and to a particular form of oratory in which distraction of attention was the predominant feature.
Clostridium difficile	Clostridium difficile colitis (also known as C. diff diarrhea, Clostridium difficile infection [CDI] and pseudomembranous colitis) is a cause of infectious diarrhea due to a type of spore-forming bacteria. Latent symptoms of CDI often mimic some flu-like symptoms and can mimic disease flare in people with inflammatory bowel disease-associated colitis. C diff release toxins that can cause bloating and diarrhea, with abdominal pain, which may become severe.
Rehydration	The management of dehydration typically involves the use of oral rehydration solution . Standard home solutions such as salted rice water, salted yogurt drinks, vegetable and chicken soups with salt can be given. Home solutions such as water in which cereal has been cooked, unsalted soup, green coconut water, weak tea (unsweetened), and unsweetened fresh fruit juices can have from half a teaspoon to full teaspoon of salt (from one-and-a-half to three grams) added per liter.
Anticholinergic	An anticholinergic agent is a substance that blocks the neurotransmitter acetylcholine in the central and the peripheral nervous system. Anticholinergics inhibit parasympathetic nerve impulses by selectively blocking the binding of the neurotransmitter acetylcholine to its receptor in nerve cells. The nerve fibers of the parasympathetic system are responsible for the involuntary movement of smooth muscles present in the gastrointestinal tract, urinary tract, lungs, etc.
Aprepitant	Aprepitant (Emend (US, EU)) is an antiemetic chemical compound that belongs to a class of drugs called substance P antagonists (SPA). It mediates its effect by blocking the neurokinin 1 (NK_1) receptor. Aprepitant is manufactured by Merck & Co. under the brand name Emend for prevention of acute and delayed chemotherapy-induced nausea and vomiting (CINV) and for prevention of postoperative nausea and vomiting.
Dolasetron	Dolasetron (trade name Anzemet) is a serotonin 5-HT_3 receptor antagonist used to treat nausea and vomiting following chemotherapy.

	Its main effect is to reduce the activity of the vagus nerve, which is a nerve that activates the vomiting center in the medulla oblongata. It does not have much antiemetic effect when symptoms are due to motion sickness.
Metoclopramide	Metoclopramide is an antiemetic and gastroprokinetic agent. It belongs to a group of medicines called ´dopaminergic´ blockers. It is commonly used to treat nausea and vomiting, to facilitate gastric emptying in people with gastroparesis, and as a treatment for the gastric stasis often associated with migraine headaches.
Ondansetron	Ondansetron is a serotonin 5-HT$_3$ receptor antagonist used mainly as an antiemetic (to treat nausea and vomiting), often following chemotherapy. It affects both peripheral and central nerves. Ondansetron reduces the activity of the vagus nerve, which deactivates the vomiting center in the medulla oblongata, and also blocks serotonin receptors in the chemoreceptor trigger zone.
Scopolamine	Scopolamine, also known as levo-duboisine and hyoscine, sold as Scopoderm, is a tropane alkaloid drug with muscarinic antagonist effects. It is among the secondary metabolites of plants from Solanaceae (nightshade) family of plants, such as henbane, jimson weed (Datura), angel's trumpets (Brugmansia), and corkwood (Duboisia). Scopolamine exerts its effects by acting as a competitive antagonist at muscarinic acetylcholine receptors, specifically M1 receptors; it is thus classified as an anticholinergic, antimuscarinic drug.
Antiemetic	An antiemetic is a drug that is effective against vomiting and nausea. Antiemetics are typically used to treat motion sickness and the side effects of opioid analgesics, general anaesthetics, and chemotherapy directed against cancer. Anti-emetics are also used for morning sickness, but there is little information about the effect on the fetus, and doctors prefer not to use them unless it is strictly necessary.
Receptor antagonist	A receptor antagonist is a type of receptor ligand or drug that does not provoke a biological response itself upon binding to a receptor, but blocks or dampens agonist-mediated responses. In pharmacology, antagonists have affinity but no efficacy for their cognate receptors, and binding will disrupt the interaction and inhibit the function of an agonist or inverse agonist at receptors. Antagonists mediate their effects by binding to the active site or to allosteric sites on receptors, or they may interact at unique binding sites not normally involved in the biological regulation of the receptor's activity.
Postoperative nausea and vomiting	Postoperative nausea and vomiting is an unpleasant complication affecting about a third of the 10% of the population undergoing general anaesthesia each year. A 2008 study compared 121 Japanese patients who experienced PONV after being given the general anesthetic propofol to 790 people who were free of post-operative nausea after receiving it.

7. UNIT-7 Gastrointestinal Agents,

Alosetron	Alosetron hydrochloride (initial brand name: Lotronex; originator: GSK) is a 5-HT$_3$ antagonist used for the management of severe diarrhea-predominant irritable bowel syndrome (IBS) in women only. It is currently marketed by Prometheus Laboratories Inc. (San Diego), also under the trade name Lotronex.
Misoprostol	Misoprostol is a synthetic prostaglandin E$_1$ (PGE$_1$) analog that is used for the prevention of nonsteroidal anti-inflammatory drug (NSAID) induced gastric ulcers, to treat missed miscarriage, to induce labor, and as an abortifacient. The latter use is controversial in the United States. Misoprostol was invented and marketed by G.D. Searle & Company (now Pfizer) under the trade name Cytotec, but other brand-name and generic formulations are now available as well.
Simethicone	Simethicone is an orally administered anti-foaming agent used to reduce bloating, discomfort or pain caused by excessive gas -- mainly swallowed air, with small amounts of hydrogen and methane-- in the stomach or intestines. Simethicone is a mixture of polydimethylsiloxane and hydrated silica gel.
Sucralfate	Sucralfate is a cytoprotective agent, an oral gastrointestinal medication primarily indicated for the treatment of active duodenal ulcers. Brand names include Sucramal in Italy; Carafate in U.S.A.; Pepsigard, Sucral, Sucrafil, Hapifate in India; Sutra or Musin in parts of South-East Asia; Sulcrate in Canada; Ulsanic in South Africa and Israel; and Antepsin in Turkey. Sucralfate is also used for the treatment of gastroesophageal reflux disease (GERD) and stress ulcers. Unlike the other classes of medications used for treatment of peptic ulcers, sucralfate is a sucrose sulfate-aluminium complex that binds to the mucosa, thus creating a physical barrier that impairs diffusion of hydrochloric acid in the gastrointestinal tract and prevents degradation of mucus by acid. It also stimulates bicarbonate output and acts like an acid buffer with cytoprotective properties.
Ursodiol	Ursodiol, also known as ursodeoxycholic acid and the abbreviation UDCA, is one of the secondary bile acids, which are metabolic byproducts of intestinal bacteria.

7. UNIT-7 Gastrointestinal Agents,

CHAPTER QUIZ: KEY TERMS, PEOPLE, PLACES, CONCEPTS

1. A _____ is any of various colorless, odorless, light mixtures of alkanes in the C15 to C40 range from a non-vegetable (mineral) source, particularly a distillate of petroleum.

   The name _____ by itself is imprecise, having been used to label many specific oils over the past few centuries. Other names, similarly imprecise, include white oil, liquid paraffin, and liquid petroleum.

   a. Homeopathic
   b. Mineral oil
   c. Chiropractic
   d. Serutan

2. An _____ agent is a substance that blocks the neurotransmitter acetylcholine in the central and the peripheral nervous system. _____s inhibit parasympathetic nerve impulses by selectively blocking the binding of the neurotransmitter acetylcholine to its receptor in nerve cells. The nerve fibers of the parasympathetic system are responsible for the involuntary movement of smooth muscles present in the gastrointestinal tract, urinary tract, lungs, etc.

   a. Ambutonium bromide
   b. Anticholinergic
   c. Oxapium iodide
   d. Oxitropium bromide

3. _____, or Ispaghula, is the common name used for several members of the plant genus Plantago whose seeds are used commercially for the production of mucilage.

   a. Psyllium
   b. Rauvolfia
   c. Red raspberry leaf
   d. Rhamnus cathartica

4. An _____ is a substance which neutralizes stomach acidity.

   a. Calcium carbonate
   b. Magnesium oxide
   c. Antacid
   d. Pepto-Bismol

5. . _____ is an antiemetic and gastroprokinetic agent. It belongs to a group of medicines called ´dopaminergic´ blockers. It is commonly used to treat nausea and vomiting, to facilitate gastric emptying in people with gastroparesis, and as a treatment for the gastric stasis often associated with migraine headaches.

   a. Metoclopramide
   b. Naloxone
   c. Nevirapine

1. b
2. b
3. a
4. c
5. a

You can take the complete Online Interactive Chapter Practice Test

for 7. UNIT-7 Gastrointestinal Agents,
on all key terms, persons, places, and concepts.

No Additional Costs

http://www.Cram101.com

Register, send an email request to Travis.Reese@Cram101.com to get your user Id and password.

Include your customer order number, and ISBN number from your studyguide Retailer.

8. UNIT-8 Renal/Genitourinary Agents,

CHAPTER OUTLINE: KEY TERMS, PEOPLE, PLACES, CONCEPTS

Amiloride

Bumetanide

Ethacrynic acid

Metolazone

Thiazide

Torasemide

Triamterene

Mechanism of action

Eplerenone

Sodium channel blocker

Chlorthalidone

Doxazosin

Osmotic diuretic

Hyperkalemia

Combination

Pharmacokinetics

Alfuzosin

Alprostadil

Avanafil

Benign prostatic hyperplasia

Dutasteride

	Finasteride
	Phosphodiesterase inhibitor
	Sildenafil
	Tadalafil
	Vardenafil
	Yohimbine
	Silodosin
	Phenazopyridine
	Urinary incontinence
	Urinary
	Urge incontinence

CHAPTER HIGHLIGHTS & NOTES: KEY TERMS, PEOPLE, PLACES, CONCEPTS

Amiloride	Amiloride is a potassium-sparing diuretic, first approved for use in 1967, used in the management of hypertension and congestive heart failure. Amiloride was also tested as treatment of cystic fibrosis, but it was revealed inefficient in vivo due to its short time of action, therefore longer-acting ENaC inhibitors may prove more effective, e.g. Benzamil.
Bumetanide	Bumetanide is a loop diuretic of the sulfamyl category to treat heart failure. It is often used in people in whom high doses of furosemide are ineffective. It is marketed by Hoffmann-La Roche.
Ethacrynic acid	Etacrynic acid (INN) or ethacrynic acid trade name Edecrin, is a loop diuretic used to treat high blood pressure and the swelling caused by diseases like congestive heart failure, liver failure, and kidney failure.

	Unlike the other loop diuretics, etacrynic acid is not a sulfonamide and thus, its use is not contraindicated in those with sulfa allergies. Etacrynic acid is a phenoxyacetic acid derivative containing a ketone group and a methylene group.
Metolazone	Metolazone is a thiazide-like diuretic marketed under the brand names Zytanix from Zydus Cadila, Zaroxolyn, and Mykrox. It is primarily used to treat congestive heart failure and high blood pressure. Metolazone indirectly decreases the amount of water reabsorbed into the bloodstream by the kidney, so that blood volume decreases and urine volume increases.
Thiazide	Thiazide is a type of molecule and a class of diuretics often used to treat hypertension (high blood pressure) and edema (such as that caused by heart, liver, or kidney disease). The thiazides and thiazide-like diuretics reduce the risk of death, stroke, heart attack and heart failure due to hypertension. In most countries, the thiazides are the cheapest antihypertensive drugs available.
Torasemide	Torasemide (rINN) or torsemide (USAN) is a pyridine-sulfonyl urea type loop diuretic mainly used in the management of edema associated with congestive heart failure. It is also used at low doses for the management of hypertension. It is marketed under the brand name Demadex, Diuver and Examide. Compared to other loop diuretics, torasemide has a more prolonged diuretic effect than equipotent doses of furosemide and relatively decreased potassium-loss. There is no evidence of torasemide-induced ototoxicity demonstrated in humans.
Triamterene	Triamterene is a potassium-sparing diuretic used in combination with thiazide diuretics for the treatment of hypertension and edema. In combination with hydrochlorothiazide, it is marketed under the names Maxzide and Dyazide.
Mechanism of action	In pharmacology, the term mechanism of action refers to the specific biochemical interaction through which a drug substance produces its pharmacological effect. A mechanism of action usually includes mention of the specific molecular targets to which the drug binds, such as an enzyme or receptor. For example, the mechanism of action of aspirin involves irreversible inhibition of the enzyme cyclooxygenase, therefore suppressing the production of prostaglandins and thromboxanes, thereby reducing pain and inflammation.

8. UNIT-8 Renal/Genitourinary Agents,

Eplerenone	Eplerenone (INN) is an aldosterone antagonist used as an adjunct in the management of chronic heart failure. It is similar to the diuretic spironolactone, though it is much more selective for the mineralocorticoid receptor in comparison (i.e., does not possess any antiandrogen, progestogen, or estrogenic effects), and is specifically marketed for reducing cardiovascular risk in patients following myocardial infarction. It is marketed by Pfizer under the trade name Inspra.
Sodium channel blocker	Sodium channel blockers are agents that impair conduction of sodium ions through sodium channels.
Chlorthalidone	Chlortalidone or chlorthalidone is a diuretic drug used to treat hypertension, originally marketed as Hygroton in the USA. It is described as a thiazide diuretic (or, rather, a thiazide-like diuretic because it acts similarly to the thiazides but does not contain the benzothiadiazine molecular structure). Compared with other medications of the thiazide class, chlortalidone has the longest duration of action but a similar diuretic effect at maximal therapeutic doses. It is often used in the management of hypertension and edema.
Doxazosin	Doxazosin mesylate, a quinazoline compound sold by Pfizer under the brand names Cardura and Carduran, is an α1-selective alpha blocker used to treat high blood pressure and urinary retention associated with benign prostatic hyperplasia (BPH). On February 22, 2005, the US FDA approved a sustained release form of doxazosin, to be marketed as Cardura XL. It is an alpha-1 adrenergic receptor blocker that inhibits the binding of norepinephrine (released from sympathetic nerve terminals) to the alpha-1 receptors on the membrane of vascular smooth muscle cells. The primary effect of this inhibition is relaxed vascular smooth muscle tone (vasodilation), which decreases peripheral vascular resistance, leading to decreased blood pressure.
Osmotic diuretic	An osmotic diuretic is a type of diuretic that inhibits reabsorption of water and sodium. They are pharmacologically inert substances that are given intravenously. They increase the osmolarity of blood and renal filtrate.
Hyperkalemia	Hyperkalemia refers to the condition in which the concentration of the electrolyte potassium (K^+) in the blood is elevated. The symptoms of elevated potassium are nonspecific, and the condition is usually discovered on blood tests performed for another reason. Extreme hyperkalemia is a medical emergency due to the risk of potentially fatal abnormal heart rhythms (arrhythmia).
Combination	In mathematics, a combination is a way of selecting members from a grouping, such that the order of selection does not matter. In smaller cases it is possible to count the number of combinations.

Pharmacokinetics	Pharmacokinetics, is a branch of pharmacology dedicated to the determination of the fate of substances administered externally to a living organism. The substances of interest include pharmaceutical agents, hormones, nutrients, and toxins. Pharmacokinetics includes the study of the mechanisms of absorption and distribution of an administered drug, the chemical changes of the substance in the body (e.g. by metabolic enzymes such as CYP or UGT enzymes), and the effects and routes of excretion of the metabolites of the drug.
Alfuzosin	Alfuzosin is an α_1 receptor antagonist used to treat benign prostatic hyperplasia (BPH). It works by relaxing the muscles in the prostate and bladder neck, making it easier to urinate. Alfuzosin is marketed in the United States by Sanofi Aventis under the brand name Uroxatral and elsewhere under the tradename Xatral, and in Egypt under name of Prostetrol.
Alprostadil	Prostaglandin E_1, known pharmaceutically as alprostadil, is a prostaglandin. It is a drug used in the treatment of erectile dysfunction and has vasodilatory properties. http://cat.sagepub.com/content/16/3/326
Avanafil	Avanafil is a PDE5 inhibitor approved for erectile dysfunction on April 27, 2012. Avanafil is known by the trademark name Stendra and was developed by Vivus Inc. It acts by inhibiting a specific phosphodiesterase type 5 enzyme which is found in various body tissues, but primarily in the corpus cavernosum penis, as well as the retina. Other similar drugs are sildenafil, tadalafil and vardenafil.
Benign prostatic hyperplasia	Benign prostatic hyperplasia, also called benign enlargement of the prostate (BEP), adenofibromyomatous hyperplasia and benign prostatic hypertrophy (technically incorrect usage), is a benign increase in size of the prostate. Benign prostatic hyperplasia involves hyperplasia of prostatic stromal and epithelial cells, resulting in the formation of large, fairly discrete nodules in the periurethral region (transition zone) of the prostate. When sufficiently large, the nodules impinge on the urethra and increase resistance to flow of urine from the bladder.
Dutasteride	Dutasteride is a dual 5-a reductase inhibitor that inhibits conversion of testosterone to dihydrotestosterone (DHT). It is used for benign prostatic hyperplasia however increases the risk of erectile dysfunction and decrease sexual desire.
Finasteride	Finasteride is a synthetic drug for the treatment of benign prostatic hyperplasia (BPH) and male pattern baldness (MPB). It is a type II 5a-reductase inhibitor. 5a-reductase is an enzyme that converts testosterone to dihydrotestosterone (DHT).

8. UNIT-8 Renal/Genitourinary Agents,

Phosphodiesterase inhibitor	A phosphodiesterase inhibitor is a drug that blocks one or more of the five subtypes of the enzyme phosphodiesterase, thereby preventing the inactivation of the intracellular second messengers cyclic adenosine monophosphate (cAMP) and cyclic guanosine monophosphate (cGMP) by the respective PDE subtype(s).
Sildenafil	Sildenafil citrate, sold as Viagra, Revatio and under various other trade names, is a drug used to treat erectile dysfunction and pulmonary arterial hypertension (PAH). It was originally developed by British scientists and then brought to market by the US-based pharmaceutical company Pfizer. It acts by inhibiting cGMP-specific phosphodiesterase type 5, an enzyme that promotes degradation of cGMP, which regulates blood flow in the penis.
Tadalafil	Tadalafil is a PDE5 inhibitor marketed in pill form for treating erectile dysfunction (ED) under the name Cialis, and under the name Adcirca for the treatment of pulmonary arterial hypertension. In October 2011 the U.S. Food and Drug Administration (FDA) approved Cialis for treatment the signs and symptoms of benign prostatic hyperplasia (BPH) as well as a combination of BPH and erectile dysfunction (ED) when the conditions coincide. It initially was developed by the biotechnology company ICOS, and then again developed and marketed world-wide by Lilly ICOS, LLC, the joint venture of ICOS Corporation and Eli Lilly and Company.
Vardenafil	Vardenafil (INN) is a PDE5 inhibitor used for treating erectile dysfunction that is sold under the trade names Levitra and Staxyn. Vardenafil was co-marketed by Bayer Pharmaceuticals, GlaxoSmithKline, and Schering-Plough under the trade name Levitra. As of 2005, the co-promotion rights of GSK on Levitra have been returned to Bayer in many markets outside the U.S. In Italy, Bayer sells vardenafil as Levitra and GSK sells it as Vivanza.
Yohimbine	Yohimbine common brand names are: Erex, Testomar, Yocon, Yohimar, Yohimbe. It is a stimulant with aphrodisiac and mild MAOI effects that primarily acts as an antagonist of a_2 receptors. It is sometimes sold as prescription medicine in pure form for the treatment of xerostomia and sexual dysfunction.
Silodosin	Silodosin (trade names Rapaflo (USA), Silodyx (Europe), Rapilif (India), Silodal (India), Urief) is a medication for the symptomatic treatment of benign prostatic hyperplasia. It acts as an a_1-adrenoceptor antagonist with high uroselectivity (selectivity for the prostate). Silodosin received its first marketing approval in Japan in May 2006 under the tradename Urief, which is jointly marketed by Kissei Pharmaceutical Co., Ltd.
Phenazopyridine	Phenazopyridine is a chemical which, when excreted into the urine, has a local analgesic effect. It is often used to alleviate the pain, irritation, discomfort, or urgency caused by urinary tract infections, surgery, or injury to the urinary tract.

Urinary incontinence	Urinary incontinence, involuntary urination, is any leakage of urine or fecal matter. It can be a common and distressing problem, which may have a profound impact on quality of life. Urinary incontinence almost always results from an underlying treatable medical condition but is under-reported to medical practitioners.
Urinary	The urinary system or renal system is the organ system that produces, stores, and eliminates urine. In humans it includes two kidneys, two ureters, the bladder and the urethra. The female and male urinary system are very similar, differing only in the length of the urethra.
Urge incontinence	Urge incontinence is a form of urinary incontinence characterized by the involuntary loss of urine occurring for no apparent reason while feeling urinary urgency, a sudden need or urge to urinate.

1. _____ is a potassium-sparing diuretic used in combination with thiazide diuretics for the treatment of hypertension and edema. In combination with hydrochlorothiazide, it is marketed under the names Maxzide and Dyazide.

   a. Triamterene
   b. Pteridine
   c. Triamterene
   d. Biopterin

2. _____, also called benign enlargement of the prostate (BEP), adenofibromyomatous hyperplasia and benign prostatic hypertrophy (technically incorrect usage), is a benign increase in size of the prostate.

   _____ involves hyperplasia of prostatic stromal and epithelial cells, resulting in the formation of large, fairly discrete nodules in the periurethral region (transition zone) of the prostate. When sufficiently large, the nodules impinge on the urethra and increase resistance to flow of urine from the bladder.

   a. prostatic hyperplasia
   b. Homeopathic
   c. Chiropractic
   d. Benign prostatic hyperplasia

3. . _____, involuntary urination, is any leakage of urine or fecal matter. It can be a common and distressing problem, which may have a profound impact on quality of life. _____ almost always results from an underlying treatable medical condition but is under-reported to medical practitioners.

   a. Urinary incontinence

8. UNIT-8 Renal/Genitourinary Agents,

b. isomer

c. Orphan Drug Act

d. Tykerb

4. In mathematics, a _____ is a way of selecting members from a grouping, such that the order of selection does not matter. In smaller cases it is possible to count the number of _____s. For example given three fruits, say an apple, an orange and a pear, there are three _____s of two that can be drawn from this set: an apple and a pear; an apple and an orange; or a pear and an orange.

a. Homeopathic

b. Combination

c. International unit

d. Intrinsic activity

5. _____ is a form of urinary incontinence characterized by the involuntary loss of urine occurring for no apparent reason while feeling urinary urgency, a sudden need or urge to urinate.

a. Urge incontinence

b. Orphan Drug Act

c. Esomeprazole

d. Tykerb

ANSWER KEY
8. UNIT-8 Renal/Genitourinary Agents,

1. c
2. d
3. a
4. b
5. a

You can take the complete Online Interactive Chapter Practice Test

for 8. UNIT-8 Renal/Genitourinary Agents,
on all key terms, persons, places, and concepts.

No Additional Costs

http://www.Cram101.com

Register, send an email request to Travis.Reese@Cram101.com to get your user Id and password.

Include your customer order number, and ISBN number from your studyguide Retailer.

9. UNIT-9 Musculoskeletal Agents,

CHAPTER OUTLINE: KEY TERMS, PEOPLE, PLACES, CONCEPTS

Antipyretic

Celecoxib

Etodolac

Indometacin

Ketoprofen

Mefenamic acid

Meloxicam

Nabumetone

Naproxen

Oxaprozin

Sulindac

Inflammation

Osteoarthritis

Arthritis

Tolmetin

Pharmacokinetics

Anakinra

Antimalarial

Etanercept

Infliximab

Sulfonamide

Mechanism of action

Hydroxychloroquine

Methotrexate

Allopurinol

Colchicine

Febuxostat

Hyperuricemia

Gout

Sulfinpyrazone

Asymptomatic

Alendronic acid

Denosumab

Hormone replacement therapy

Osteoporosis

Selective estrogen receptor modulators

Zoledronic acid

Parathyroid hormone

Baclofen

Benzodiazepine

Carisoprodol

Cyclobenzaprine

9. UNIT-9 Musculoskeletal Agents,

CHAPTER OUTLINE: KEY TERMS, PEOPLE, PLACES, CONCEPTS

Muscle relaxant

Tizanidine

Tricyclic antidepressants

CHAPTER HIGHLIGHTS & NOTES: KEY TERMS, PEOPLE, PLACES, CONCEPTS

Antipyretic	Antipyretics against, and pyreticus, pertaining to fever, are substances that reduce fever. Antipyretics cause the hypothalamus to override an interleukin-induced increase in temperature. The body then works to lower the temperature, resulting in a reduction in fever.
Celecoxib	Celecoxib INN is a sulfonamide nonsteroidal anti-inflammatory drug (NSAID) and selective COX-2 inhibitor used in the treatment of osteoarthritis, rheumatoid arthritis, acute pain, painful menstruation and menstrual symptoms, and to reduce numbers of colon and rectum polyps in patients with familial adenomatous polyposis. Celecoxib is licensed for use in osteoarthritis, rheumatoid arthritis, acute pain, painful menstruation and menstrual symptoms, ankylosing spondylitis, and to reduce the number of colon and rectal polyps in patients with familial adenomatous polyposis. It was originally intended to relieve pain while minimizing the gastrointestinal adverse effects usually seen with conventional NSAIDs. In practice, its primary indication is in patients who need regular and long-term pain relief; there is probably no advantage to using celecoxib for short term or acute pain relief over conventional NSAIDs, except in the situation where nonselective NSAIDs or aspirin cause cutaneous reactions (urticaria or 'hives').
Etodolac	Etodolac is a nonsteroidal anti-inflammatory drug . The U.S. Food and Drug Administration approved etodolac in January 1991.
Indometacin	Indometacin (INN) or indomethacin is a non-steroidal anti-inflammatory drug (NSAID) commonly used as a prescription medication to reduce fever, pain, stiffness, and swelling. It works by inhibiting the production of prostaglandins, molecules known to cause these symptoms. It is marketed under more than seventy different trade names.
Ketoprofen	Ketoprofen, 2-(3-benzoylphenyl)-propionic acid (chemical formula $C_{16}H_{14}O_3$) is one of the propionic acid class of nonsteroidal anti-inflammatory drug (NSAID) with analgesic and antipyretic effects.

9. UNIT-9 Musculoskeletal Agents,

	It acts by inhibiting the body's production of prostaglandin.
Mefenamic acid	Mefenamic acid is a non-steroidal anti-inflammatory drug used to treat pain, including menstrual pain. It is typically prescribed for oral administration. Mefenamic acid is marketed in the USA as Ponstel and is commonly known in UK as Ponstan.
Meloxicam	Meloxicam is a nonsteroidal anti-inflammatory drug (NSAID) with analgesic and fever reducer effects. It is a derivative of oxicam, closely related to piroxicam, and falls in the enolic acid group of NSAIDs. It was developed by Boehringer-Ingelheim.
Nabumetone	Nabumetone is a non-steroidal anti-inflammatory drug (NSAID), the only 1-naphthaleneacetic acid derivative. Nabumetone has been developed by Beecham. It is available under numerous brand names, such as Relafen, Relifex and Gambaran.
Naproxen	Naproxen sodium (INN) is a nonsteroidal anti-inflammatory drug (NSAID). Naproxen and naproxen sodium are marketed under various trade names, including: Aleve, Anaprox, Antalgin, Apranax, Feminax Ultra, Flanax, Inza, Midol Extended Relief, Nalgesin, Naposin, Naprelan, Naprogesic, Naprosyn, Narocin, Proxen, Soproxen, Synflex and Xenobid. Naproxen was originally marketed as the prescription drug Naprosyn by Syntex in 1976, and naproxen sodium was first marketed under the trade name Anaprox in 1980. It remains a prescription-only drug in much of the world.
Oxaprozin	Oxaprozin, (sold under the names: Daypro, Dayrun, Duraprox) is a non-steroidal anti-inflammatory drug (NSAID), used to relieve the inflammation, swelling, stiffness, and joint pain associated with osteoarthritis and rheumatoid arthritis. Chemically, it is a propionic acid derivative. It is available in 600 mg tablets.
Sulindac	Sulindac is a non-steroidal anti-inflammatory drug of the arylalkanoic acid class that is marketed in the UK & U.S. by Merck as Clinoril.
Inflammation	Inflammation is part of the complex biological response of vascular tissues to harmful stimuli, such as pathogens, damaged cells, or irritants. The classical signs of acute inflammation are pain, heat, redness, swelling, and loss of function. Inflammation is a protective attempt by the organism to remove the injurious stimuli and to initiate the healing process.
Osteoarthritis	Osteoarthritis also known as degenerative arthritis or degenerative joint disease or osteoarthrosis, is a group of mechanical abnormalities involving degradation of joints, including articular cartilage and subchondral bone. Symptoms may include joint pain, tenderness, stiffness, locking, and sometimes an effusion. A variety of causes-hereditary, developmental, metabolic, and mechanical deficits-may initiate processes leading to loss of cartilage.
Arthritis	Arthritis is a form of joint disorder that involves inflammation of one or more joints.

	There are over 100 different forms of arthritis. The most common form, osteoarthritis is a result of trauma to the joint, infection of the joint, or age.
Tolmetin	Tolmetin is a non-steroidal anti-inflammatory drug of the arylalkanoic acids. It is used primarily to reduce hormones that cause pain, swelling, tenderness, and stiffness in conditions such as osteoarthritis and rheumatoid arthritis, including juvenile rheumatoid arthritis. In the United States it is marketed as Tolectin and comes as a tablet or capsule.
Pharmacokinetics	Pharmacokinetics, is a branch of pharmacology dedicated to the determination of the fate of substances administered externally to a living organism. The substances of interest include pharmaceutical agents, hormones, nutrients, and toxins.
	Pharmacokinetics includes the study of the mechanisms of absorption and distribution of an administered drug, the chemical changes of the substance in the body (e.g. by metabolic enzymes such as CYP or UGT enzymes), and the effects and routes of excretion of the metabolites of the drug.
Anakinra	Anakinra is a drug used to treat rheumatoid arthritis. It is an interleukin-1 (IL-1) receptor antagonist.
Antimalarial	Antimalarial medications, also known as antimalarials, are designed to prevent or cure malaria. Such drugs may be used for some or all of the following:•Treatment of malaria in individuals with suspected or confirmed infection•Prevention of infection in individuals visiting a malaria-endemic region who have no immunity (Malaria prophylaxis)•Routine intermittent treatment of certain groups in endemic regions (Intermittent preventive therapy)
	Some antimalarial agents, particularly chloroquine and hydroxychloroquine, are also used in the treatment of rheumatoid arthritis and lupus-associated arthritis.
	Current practice in treating cases of malaria is based on the concept of combination therapy, since this offers several advantages, including reduced risk of treatment failure, reduced risk of developing resistance, enhanced convenience, and reduced side-effects.
Etanercept	Etanercept (trade name Enbrel) is a biopharmaceutical that treats autoimmune diseases by interfering with tumor necrosis factor (TNF; a soluble inflammatory cytokine) by acting as a TNF inhibitor. It has U.S. F.D.A. approval to treat rheumatoid, juvenile rheumatoid and psoriatic arthritis, plaque psoriasis and ankylosing spondylitis. TNF-alpha is the 'master regulator' of the inflammatory (immune) response in many organ systems.
Infliximab	Infliximab is a monoclonal antibody against tumour necrosis factor alpha (TNF-α) used to treat autoimmune diseases. Remicade is marketed by Janssen Biotech, Inc. (formerly Centocor Biotech, Inc).

9. UNIT-9 Musculoskeletal Agents,

Sulfonamide	Sulfonamide or sulphonamide is the basis of several groups of drugs. The original antibacterial sulfonamides (sometimes called sulfa drugs or sulpha drugs) are synthetic antimicrobial agents that contain the sulfonamide group. Some sulfonamides are also devoid of antibacterial activity, e.g., the anticonvulsant sultiame.
Mechanism of action	In pharmacology, the term mechanism of action refers to the specific biochemical interaction through which a drug substance produces its pharmacological effect. A mechanism of action usually includes mention of the specific molecular targets to which the drug binds, such as an enzyme or receptor. For example, the mechanism of action of aspirin involves irreversible inhibition of the enzyme cyclooxygenase, therefore suppressing the production of prostaglandins and thromboxanes, thereby reducing pain and inflammation.
Hydroxychloroquine	Hydroxychloroquine is an antimalarial drug, sold under the trade names Plaquenil, Axemal (in India), Dolquine, and Quensyl, also used to reduce inflammation in the treatment of rheumatoid arthritis and lupus. Hydroxychloroquine differs from chloroquine by the presence of a hydroxyl group at the end of the side chain: The N-ethyl substituent is beta-hydroxylated. It is available for oral administration as hydroxychloroquine sulfate (plaquenil) of which 200 mg contains 155 mg base in chiral form.
Methotrexate	Methotrexate (rINN), abbreviated MTX and formerly known as amethopterin, is an antimetabolite and antifolate drug. It is used in treatment of cancer, autoimmune diseases, ectopic pregnancy, and for the induction of medical abortions. It acts by inhibiting the metabolism of folic acid.
Allopurinol	Allopurinol is a drug used primarily to treat hyperuricemia (excess uric acid in blood plasma) and its complications, including chronic gout. It is a xanthine oxidase inhibitor which is administered orally.
Colchicine	Colchicine is a medication that treats gout. It is a toxic natural product and secondary metabolite, originally extracted from plants of the genus Colchicum (autumn crocus, Colchicum autumnale, also known as 'meadow saffron'). It was used originally to treat rheumatic complaints, especially gout, and still finds use for these purposes today despite dosing issues concerning its toxicity. It was also prescribed for its cathartic and emetic effects.
Febuxostat	Febuxostat is a urate lowering drug, an inhibitor of xanthine oxidase that is indicated for use in the treatment of hyperuricemia and gout. Febuxostat received marketing approval by the European Medicines Agency on April 21, 2008 and was approved by the U.S. Food and Drug Administration on February 16, 2009.

Hyperuricemia	Hyperuricemia is a level of uric acid in the blood that is abnormally high. In humans, the upper end of the normal range is 360 μmol/L (6 mg/dL) for women and 400 μmol/L (6.8 mg/dL) for men.
Gout	Gout is a medical condition usually characterized by recurrent attacks of acute inflammatory arthritis-a red, tender, hot, swollen joint. The metatarsal-phalangeal joint at the base of the big toe is the most commonly affected (approximately 50% of cases). However, it may also present as tophi, kidney stones, or urate nephropathy.
Sulfinpyrazone	Sulfinpyrazone is a uricosuric medication used to treat gout. It also sometimes is used to reduce platelet aggregation by inhibiting degranulation of platelets which reduces the release of ADP and thromboxane. Like other uricosurics, sulfinpyrazone works by competitively inhibiting uric acid reabsorption in the proximal tubule of the kidney.
Asymptomatic	In medicine, a disease is considered asymptomatic if a patient is a carrier for a disease or infection but experiences no symptoms. A condition might be asymptomatic if it fails to show the noticeable symptoms with which it is usually associated. Asymptomatic infections are also called subclinical infections.
Alendronic acid	Alendronic acid (INN) or alendronate sodium (USAN) - sold as Fosamax by Merck - is a bisphosphonate drug used for osteoporosis and several other bone diseases. It is marketed alone as well as in combination with vitamin D (2,800 IU and 5600 IU, under the name Fosamax+D). Merck's U.S. patent on alendronate expired in 2008 and Merck lost a series of appeals to block a generic version of the drug from being certified by the U.S. Food and Drug Administration (FDA).
Denosumab	Denosumab is a fully human monoclonal antibody for the treatment of osteoporosis, treatment-induced bone loss, bone metastases, rheumatoid arthritis, multiple myeloma, and giant cell tumor of bone. It was developed by the biotechnology company Amgen. Denosumab is designed to inhibit RANKL (RANK ligand), a protein that acts as the primary signal for bone removal.
Hormone replacement therapy	Hormone replacement therapy refers to any form of hormone therapy wherein the patient, in the course of medical treatment, receives hormones, either to supplement a lack of naturally occurring hormones, or to substitute other hormones for naturally occurring hormones. Common forms of hormone replacement therapy include:•Hormone replacement therapy for menopause is based on the idea that the treatment may prevent discomfort caused by diminished circulating estrogen and progesterone hormones, or in the case of the surgically or prematurely menopausal, that it may prolong life and may reduce incidence of dementia. It involves the use of one or more of a group of medications designed to artificially boost hormone levels.

9. UNIT-9 Musculoskeletal Agents,

Osteoporosis	Osteoporosis is a disease of bones that leads to an increased risk of fracture. In osteoporosis, the bone mineral density (BMD) is reduced, bone microarchitecture deteriorates, and the amount and variety of proteins in bone are altered. Osteoporosis is defined by the World Health Organization (WHO) as a bone mineral density of 2.5 standard deviations or more below the mean peak bone mass (average of young, healthy adults) as measured by dual-energy X-ray absorptiometry; the term 'established osteoporosis' includes the presence of a fragility fracture.
Selective estrogen receptor modulators	Selective estrogen receptor modulators are a class of compounds that act on the estrogen receptor. A characteristic that distinguishes these substances from pure receptor agonists and antagonists is that their action is different in various tissues, thereby granting the possibility to selectively inhibit or stimulate estrogen-like action in various tissues. Phytoserms are Selective estrogen receptor modulatorss from a botanical source.
Zoledronic acid	Zoledronic acid or zoledronate (marketed by Novartis under the trade names Zometa, Zomera, Aclasta and Reclast) is a bisphosphonate. Zometa is used to prevent skeletal fractures in patients with cancers such as multiple myeloma and prostate cancer, as well as for treating osteoporosis. It can also be used to treat hypercalcemia of malignancy and can be helpful for treating pain from bone metastases.
Parathyroid hormone	Parathyroid hormone parathormone or parathyrin, is secreted by the chief cells of the parathyroid glands as a polypeptide containing 84 amino acids. It acts to increase the concentration of calcium (Ca^{2+}) in the blood, whereas calcitonin (a hormone produced by the parafollicular cells (C cells) of the thyroid gland) acts to decrease calcium concentration. PTH acts to increase the concentration of calcium in the blood by acting upon the parathyroid hormone 1 receptor (high levels in bone and kidney) and the parathyroid hormone 2 receptor (high levels in the central nervous system, pancreas, testis, and placenta).
Baclofen	Baclofen (brand names Kemstro, Lioresal, Liofen, Gablofen, Beklo and Baclosan) is a derivative of gamma-aminobutyric acid (GABA). It is primarily used to treat spasticity and is in the early research stages for use for the treatment of alcoholism. It is also used by compounding pharmacies in topical pain creams as a muscle relaxant.
Benzodiazepine	A benzodiazepine is a psychoactive drug whose core chemical structure is the fusion of a benzene ring and a diazepine ring. The first benzodiazepine, chlordiazepoxide (Librium), was discovered accidentally by Leo Sternbach in 1955, and made available in 1960 by Hoffmann-La Roche, which has also marketed diazepam (Valium) since 1963.

Benzodiazepines enhance the effect of the neurotransmitter gamma-aminobutyric acid (GABA) at the $GABA_A$ receptor, resulting in sedative, hypnotic (sleep-inducing), anxiolytic (anti-anxiety), anticonvulsant, and muscle relaxant properties; also seen in the applied pharmacology of high doses of many shorter-acting benzodiazepines are amnesic-dissociative actions. |

CHAPTER HIGHLIGHTS & NOTES: KEY TERMS, PEOPLE, PLACES, CONCEPTS

Carisoprodol	Carisoprodol is a centrally acting skeletal muscle relaxant. It is slightly soluble in water and freely soluble in alcohol, chloroform and acetone. The drug's solubility is practically independent of pH. Carisoprodol is manufactured and marketed in the United States by Meda Pharmaceuticals under the brand name Soma, and in the United Kingdom and other countries under the brand names Sanoma and Carisoma. The drug is available by itself or mixed with aspirin, and in one preparation with codeine and caffeine, as well.
Cyclobenzaprine	Cyclobenzaprine, brand name Flexeril, is a muscle relaxant medication used to relieve skeletal muscle spasms and associated pain in acute musculoskeletal conditions. It is the most well-studied drug for this application, and it also has been used off-label for fibromyalgia treatment. A new bedtime formulation of cyclobenzaprine is under development for the management of fibromyalgia syndrome.
Muscle relaxant	A muscle relaxant is a drug which affects skeletal muscle function and decreases the muscle tone. It may be used to alleviate symptoms such as muscle spasms, pain, and hyperreflexia. The term 'muscle relaxant' is used to refer to two major therapeutic groups: neuromuscular blockers and spasmolytics.
Tizanidine	Tizanidine is a drug that is used as a muscle relaxant. It is a centrally acting α_2 adrenergic agonist. It is used to treat the spasms, cramping, and tightness of muscles caused by medical problems such as multiple sclerosis, spastic diplegia, back pain, or certain other injuries to the spine or central nervous system.
Tricyclic antidepressants	Tricyclic antidepressants are heterocyclic chemical compounds used primarily as antidepressants. The tetracyclic antidepressants (TeCAs), which contain four rings of atoms, are a closely related group of antidepressant compounds. In recent times, the TCAs have been largely replaced in clinical use in most parts of the world by newer antidepressants such as the selective serotonin reuptake inhibitors (SSRIs), serotonin-norepinephrine reuptake inhibitors (SNRIs) and the norepinephrine reuptake inhibitors (NRIs) like reboxetine which typically have more favorable side-effects profiles, though they are still sometimes prescribed for certain indications.

9. UNIT-9 Musculoskeletal Agents,

1. _____ is a form of joint disorder that involves inflammation of one or more joints. There are over 100 different forms of _____. The most common form, osteo_____ is a result of trauma to the joint, infection of the joint, or age.

   a. Homeopathic
   b. Arthritis
   c. Chiropractic
   d. Pamidronate

2. _____ refers to any form of hormone therapy wherein the patient, in the course of medical treatment, receives hormones, either to supplement a lack of naturally occurring hormones, or to substitute other hormones for naturally occurring hormones. Common forms of _____ include:•_____ for menopause is based on the idea that the treatment may prevent discomfort caused by diminished circulating estrogen and progesterone hormones, or in the case of the surgically or prematurely menopausal, that it may prolong life and may reduce incidence of dementia. It involves the use of one or more of a group of medications designed to artificially boost hormone levels.

   a. hormone replacement
   b. Homeopathic
   c. Chiropractic
   d. Hormone replacement therapy

3. _____s against, and pyreticus, pertaining to fever, are substances that reduce fever. _____s cause the hypothalamus to override an interleukin-induced increase in temperature. The body then works to lower the temperature, resulting in a reduction in fever.

   a. isomer
   b. Antipyretic
   c. Esomeprazole
   d. Epristeride

4. . _____ INN is a sulfonamide nonsteroidal anti-inflammatory drug (NSAID) and selective COX-2 inhibitor used in the treatment of osteoarthritis, rheumatoid arthritis, acute pain, painful menstruation and menstrual symptoms, and to reduce numbers of colon and rectum polyps in patients with familial adenomatous polyposis.

   _____ is licensed for use in osteoarthritis, rheumatoid arthritis, acute pain, painful menstruation and menstrual symptoms, ankylosing spondylitis, and to reduce the number of colon and rectal polyps in patients with familial adenomatous polyposis. It was originally intended to relieve pain while minimizing the gastrointestinal adverse effects usually seen with conventional NSAIDs. In practice, its primary indication is in patients who need regular and long-term pain relief; there is probably no advantage to using _____ for short term or acute pain relief over conventional NSAIDs, except in the situation where nonselective NSAIDs or aspirin cause cutaneous reactions (urticaria or 'hives').

   a. Delavirdine
   b. Celecoxib
   c. Tamsulosin

5. _____ is a nonsteroidal anti-inflammatory drug . The U.S. Food and Drug Administration approved _____ in January 1991.

   a. Etodolac

   b. Iodoacetic acid

   c. Alvimopan

   d. Entereg

1. b

2. d

3. b

4. b

5. a

You can take the complete Online Interactive Chapter Practice Test

for 9. UNIT-9 Musculoskeletal Agents,

on all key terms, persons, places, and concepts.

No Additional Costs

http://www.Cram101.com

Register, send an email request to Travis.Reese@Cram101.com to get your user Id and password.

Include your customer order number, and ISBN number from your studyguide Retailer.

CHAPTER OUTLINE: KEY TERMS, PEOPLE, PLACES, CONCEPTS

	Atomoxetine
	Dextroamphetamine
	Imipramine
	Modafinil
	Mechanism of action
	Donepezil
	Rivastigmine
	Dementia
	Morphine
	Oxycodone
	Pain management
	Pentazocine
	Tapentadol
	Tramadol
	Opium
	Addiction
	Opioid
	Analgesic
	Gabapentin
	Pregabalin
	Side effect

	Pharmacokinetics
	Almotriptan
	Cyproheptadine
	Dihydroergotamine
	Eletriptan
	Frovatriptan
	Sumatriptan
	Antiepileptic
	Carbidopa
	Dopamine agonist
	Parkinson's disease
	Pramipexole
	Rasagiline
	Selegiline
	Tolcapone
	Trihexyphenidyl
	Benztropine
	Biperiden
	Entacapone

Atomoxetine	Atomoxetine is a drug approved for the treatment of attention-deficit hyperactivity disorder (ADHD). It is a selective norepinephrine reuptake inhibitor (NRI), not to be confused with selective serotonin and norepinephrine reuptake inhibitors (SNRIs) or selective serotonin reuptake inhibitors (SSRIs), both of which are currently the most prescribed form of antidepressants. This compound is manufactured, marketed and sold in the United States under the brand name Strattera by Eli Lilly and Company as a hydrochloride salt (atomoxetine HCl), the original patent filing company, and current U.S. patent owner.
Dextroamphetamine	Dextroamphetamine is a psychostimulant drug which is known to produce increased wakefulness and focus as well as decreased fatigue and decreased appetite.
	Dextroamphetamine is the dextrorotatory, or 'right-handed', stereoisomer of the amphetamine molecule. The amphetamine molecule has two stereoisomers; levoamphetamine and dextroamphetamine.
Imipramine	Imipramine also known as melipramine, is an a tricyclic antidepressant (TCA) of the dibenzazepine group. Imipramine is mainly used in the treatment of major depression and enuresis (inability to control urination).
	It has also been evaluated for use in panic disorder.
Modafinil	Modafinil is a wakefulness-promoting drug that is approved by the United States' Food and Drug Administration (FDA) for the treatment of narcolepsy, shift work sleep disorder and excessive daytime sleepiness associated with obstructive sleep apnea.
Mechanism of action	In pharmacology, the term mechanism of action refers to the specific biochemical interaction through which a drug substance produces its pharmacological effect. A mechanism of action usually includes mention of the specific molecular targets to which the drug binds, such as an enzyme or receptor.
	For example, the mechanism of action of aspirin involves irreversible inhibition of the enzyme cyclooxygenase, therefore suppressing the production of prostaglandins and thromboxanes, thereby reducing pain and inflammation.
Donepezil	Donepezil, marketed under the trade name Aricept by its developer Eisai and partner Pfizer, is a centrally acting reversible acetylcholinesterase inhibitor. Its main therapeutic use is in the palliative treatment of mild to moderate Alzheimer's disease. Common side effects include gastrointestinal upset.
Rivastigmine	Rivastigmine is a parasympathomimetic or cholinergic agent for the treatment of mild to moderate dementia of the Alzheimer's type and dementia due to Parkinson's disease.

	The drug can be administered orally or via a transdermal patch; the latter form reduces the prevalence of side effects, which typically include nausea and vomiting. The drug is eliminated through the urine, and appears to have relatively few drug-drug interactions.
Dementia	Dementia is a broad category of brain diseases that cause long term loss of the ability to think and reason clearly that is severe enough to affect a person's daily functioning. For the diagnosis to be present it must be a change from previous baseline mental function.

The most common form of dementia is Alzheimer's disease (75%). |
| Morphine | Morphine (; MS Contin, MSIR, Avinza, Kadian, Oramorph, Roxanol, Kapanol) is a potent opiate analgesic medication and is considered to be the prototypical opioid. It was first isolated in 1804 by Friedrich Sertürner, first distributed by same in 1817, and first commercially sold by Merck in 1827, which at the time was a single small chemists' shop. It was more widely used after the invention of the hypodermic needle in 1857. It took its name from the Greek god of dreams Morpheus . |
| Oxycodone | Oxycodone is an opioid analgesic medication synthesized from opium-derived thebaine. It was developed in 1916 in Germany, as one of several new semi-synthetic opioids in an attempt to improve on the existing opioids: morphine, diacetylmorphine (heroin), and codeine.

Oxycodone oral medications are generally prescribed for the relief of moderate to severe pain. |
Pain management	Pain management is a branch of medicine employing an interdisciplinary approach for easing the suffering and improving the quality of life of those living with pain. The typical pain management team includes medical practitioners, clinical psychologists, physiotherapists, occupational therapists, physician assistants, nurse practitioners, and clinical nurse specialists. The team may also include other mental-health specialists and massage therapists.
Pentazocine	Pentazocine is a synthetically prepared prototypical mixed agonist-antagonist narcotic (opioid analgesic) drug of the benzomorphan class of opioids used to treat moderate to moderately severe pain. Pentazocine is sold under several brand names, such as Fortral, Talwin NX (with the μ-antagonist naloxone, will cause withdrawal in opioid dependent persons on injection), Talwin, Talwin PX (without naloxone), Fortwin (Lactate injectable form) and Talacen (with acetaminophen). This compound may exist as one of two enantiomers, named (+)-pentazocine and (-)-pentazocine.
Tapentadol	Tapentadol is a centrally acting analgesic with a dual mode of action as an agonist at the μ-opioid receptor and as a norepinephrine reuptake inhibitor. While its analgesic actions have been compared to tramadol and oxycodone, its general potency is somewhere between tramadol and morphine in effectiveness. Tapentadol is a new molecular entity that is structurally similar to Tramadol (Tramal).

Tramadol	Tramadol hydrochloride (Ultram, Tramal) is a centrally acting synthetic opioid analgesic used in treating severe pain. The drug has a wide range of applications, including treatment for Rheumatoid arthritis, restless legs syndrome and fibromyalgia. It was developed by the pharmaceutical company Grünenthal GmbH in the late 1970s.
Opium	Opium is the dried latex obtained from the opium poppy (Papaver somniferum). Opium contains approximately 12% of the analgesic alkaloid morphine, which is processed chemically to produce heroin and other synthetic opioids for medicinal use and for the illegal drug trade. The latex also contains the closely related opiates codeine and thebaine and non-analgesic alkaloids such as papaverine and noscapine.
Addiction	Addiction is the continued use of a mood altering substance or behavior despite adverse consequences, or a neurological impairment leading to such behaviors. Addictions can include, but are not limited to, drug abuse, exercise addiction, sexual addiction and gambling. Classic hallmarks of addiction include impaired control over substances or behavior, preoccupation with substance or behavior, continued use despite consequences, and denial.
Opioid	An opioid is a psychoactive chemical that works by binding to opioid receptors, which are found principally in the central and peripheral nervous system and the gastrointestinal tract. The receptors in these organ systems mediate both the beneficial effects and the side effects of opioids. Opioids are among the world's oldest known drugs; the therapeutic use of the opium poppy predates recorded history.
Analgesic	An analgesic is any member of the group of drugs used to achieve analgesia, relief from pain. The word analgesic derives from Greek αν - ('without') and ?λγος - ('pain'). Commonly known as painkillers, analgesic drugs act in various ways on the peripheral and central nervous systems.
Gabapentin	Gabapentin is a pharmaceutical drug, specifically a GABA analog. It was originally developed to treat epilepsy, and currently is also used to relieve neuropathic pain. There are, however, concerns regarding the quality of the trials conducted for a number of conditions.
Pregabalin	Pregabalin (INN) (Lyrica) and (Serigaptin) is an anticonvulsant drug used for neuropathic pain and as an adjunct therapy for partial seizures with or without secondary generalization in adults. It has also been found effective for generalized anxiety disorder and is (as of 2007) approved for this use in the European Union. It was designed as a more potent successor to gabapentin.

10. UNIT-10 Central Nervous System Agents,

Side effect	In medicine, a side effect is an effect, whether therapeutic or adverse, that is secondary to the one intended; although the term is predominantly employed to describe adverse effects, it can also apply to beneficial, but unintended, consequences of the use of a drug. Occasionally, drugs are prescribed or procedures performed specifically for their side effects; in that case, said side effect ceases to be a side effect, and is now an intended effect. For instance, X-rays were historically (and are currently) used as an imaging technique; the discovery of their oncolytic capability led to their employ in radiotherapy (ablation of malignant tumours).
Pharmacokinetics	Pharmacokinetics, is a branch of pharmacology dedicated to the determination of the fate of substances administered externally to a living organism. The substances of interest include pharmaceutical agents, hormones, nutrients, and toxins. Pharmacokinetics includes the study of the mechanisms of absorption and distribution of an administered drug, the chemical changes of the substance in the body (e.g. by metabolic enzymes such as CYP or UGT enzymes), and the effects and routes of excretion of the metabolites of the drug.
Almotriptan	Almotriptan (trade names Axert, Almogran (Belgium, Denmark, Finland, France, Germany, Italy, Ireland Portugal, Spain, the United Kingdom, the Netherlands, Sweden, Switzerland, South Korea...), Almotrex (Italy) and Amignul (Spain)) is a triptan drug discovered and developed by Almirall for the treatment of heavy migraine headache. It is available in 12.5 mg in most countries and also 6.25 mg in US and Canada.
Cyproheptadine	Cyproheptadine, sold under the brand name Periactin or Peritol, is a first-generation antihistamine with additional anticholinergic, antiserotonergic, and local anesthetic properties.
Dihydroergotamine	Dihydroergotamine is an ergot alkaloid used to treat migraines. It is a derivative of ergotamine. It is administered as a nasal spray or injection and has an efficacy similar to that of sumatriptan.
Eletriptan	Eletriptan (trade name Relpax, used in the form of eletriptan hydrobromide) is a second generation triptan drug intended for treatment of migraine headaches. It is used as an abortive medication, blocking a migraine attack which is already in progress. Eletriptan is marketed and manufactured by Pfizer Inc.
Frovatriptan	Frovatriptan is a triptan drug developed by Vernalis for the treatment of migraine headaches and for short term prevention of menstrual migraine. The product is licensed to Endo Pharmaceuticals in North America and Menarini in Europe.
Sumatriptan	Sumatriptan is a synthetic drug belonging to the triptan class, used for the treatment of migraine headaches.

	Structurally, it is an analog of the naturally occurring neuro-active alkaloids dimethyltryptamine (DMT), bufotenine, and 5-methoxy-dimethyltryptamine, with an N-methyl sulfonamidomethyl- group at position C-5 on the indole ring.
	Sumatriptan is produced and marketed by various drug manufacturers with many different trade names such as Sumatriptan, Imitrex, Treximet, Imigran, Imigran recovery.
Antiepileptic	Anticonvulsants (also commonly known as antiepileptic drugs or as antiseizure drugs) are a diverse group of pharmaceuticals used in the treatment of epileptic seizures. Anticonvulsants are also increasingly being used in the treatment of bipolar disorder, since many seem to act as mood stabilizers, and for the treatment of neuropathic pain. Anticonvulsants suppress the rapid and excessive firing of neurons during seizures.
Carbidopa	Carbidopa is a drug given to people with Parkinson's disease in order to inhibit peripheral metabolism of levodopa. This property is significant in that it allows a greater proportion of peripheral levodopa to cross the blood brain barrier for central nervous system effect.
Dopamine agonist	A dopamine agonist is a compound that activates dopamine receptors in the absence of dopamine. Dopamine agonists activate signaling pathways through the dopamine receptor and trimeric G-proteins, ultimately leading to changes in gene transcription.
Parkinson's disease	Parkinson's disease is a degenerative disorder of the central nervous system. The motor symptoms of Parkinson's disease result from the death of dopamine-generating cells in the substantia nigra, a region of the midbrain; the cause of this cell death is unknown. Early in the course of the disease, the most obvious symptoms are movement-related; these include shaking, rigidity, slowness of movement and difficulty with walking and gait.
Pramipexole	Pramipexole is a non-ergoline dopamine agonist indicated for treating early-stage Parkinson's disease (PD) and restless legs syndrome (RLS). It is also sometimes used off-label as a treatment for cluster headache and to counteract the problems with sexual dysfunction experienced by some users of the selective serotonin reuptake inhibitor (SSRI) antidepressants. Pramipexole has shown robust effects on pilot studies in a placebo-controlled proof of concept study in bipolar disorder.
Rasagiline	Rasagiline is an irreversible inhibitor of monoamine oxidase used as a monotherapy in early Parkinson's disease or as an adjunct therapy in more advanced cases. It is selective for MAO type B over type A by a factor of fourteen.
	It was developed by Teva Neuroscience, initially investigated by Prof.
Selegiline	Selegiline is a drug used for the treatment of early-stage Parkinson's disease, depression and senile dementia. In normal clinical doses it is a selective irreversible MAO-B inhibitor, however in larger doses it loses its specificity and also inhibits MAO-A.

10. UNIT-10 Central Nervous System Agents,

	Dietary restrictions are common for MAOI treatments, but special dietary restrictions for lower doses have been found to be unnecessary, and dietary restrictions appear to be unnecessary at standard doses when selegiline is taken as Emsam, the transdermal patch form, as no adverse events due to diet have ever been reported with Emsam. The drug was discovered by Jozsef Knoll et al. in Hungary.
Tolcapone	Tolcapone is a selective, potent and reversible nitro catechol type inhibitor of enzyme catechol-O-methyl transferase (COMT).
Trihexyphenidyl	Trihexyphenidyl also known as benzhexol, is an antiparkinsonian agent of the antimuscarinic class. It has been in clinical usage for decades. The drug is available as the hydrochloride salt.
Benztropine	Benzatropine, also known as benztropine is an anticholinergic marketed under the trade name Cogentin which is used in the treatment of Parkinson's disease, Parkinsonism, and dystonia.
Biperiden	Biperiden is an antiparkinsonian agent of the anticholinergic type. The original brand name, which still exists and is manufactured by BASFKnoll Pharma, is Akineton. Generics are available worldwide.
Entacapone	Entacapone is a drug that functions as a catechol-O-methyl transferase (COMT) inhibitor. It is used in the treatment of Parkinson's disease. When administered in conjunction with dopaminergic agents such as L-DOPA, entacapone prevents COMT from metabolizing L-DOPA into 3-methoxy-4-hydroxy-L-phenylalanine (3-OMD) in the periphery, which does not easily cross the blood brain barrier (BBB).

1. _____ is a synthetic drug belonging to the triptan class, used for the treatment of migraine headaches. Structurally, it is an analog of the naturally occurring neuro-active alkaloids dimethyltryptamine (DMT), bufotenine, and 5-methoxy-dimethyltryptamine, with an N-methyl sulfonamidomethyl- group at position C-5 on the indole ring.

   _____ is produced and marketed by various drug manufacturers with many different trade names such as _____, Imitrex, Treximet, Imigran, Imigran recovery.

   a. Lovaza
   b. Sumatriptan
   c. Nicorette
   d. Homeopathic

2. _____ is a synthetically prepared prototypical mixed agonist-antagonist narcotic (opioid analgesic) drug of the benzomorphan class of opioids used to treat moderate to moderately severe pain. _____ is sold under several brand names, such as Fortral, Talwin NX (with the μ-antagonist naloxone, will cause withdrawal in opioid dependent persons on injection), Talwin, Talwin PX (without naloxone), Fortwin (Lactate injectable form) and Talacen (with acetaminophen). This compound may exist as one of two enantiomers, named (+)-_____ and (-)-_____.

a. Phenazocine
b. Pentazocine
c. Spiradoline
d. Tifluadom

3. _____ (; MS Contin, MSIR, Avinza, Kadian, Oramorph, Roxanol, Kapanol) is a potent opiate analgesic medication and is considered to be the prototypical opioid. It was first isolated in 1804 by Friedrich Sertürner, first distributed by same in 1817, and first commercially sold by Merck in 1827, which at the time was a single small chemists' shop. It was more widely used after the invention of the hypodermic needle in 1857. It took its name from the Greek god of dreams Morpheus .

a. Morphine
b. Morphinone
c. MT-45
d. Myrophine

4. _____ is a drug approved for the treatment of attention-deficit hyperactivity disorder (ADHD). It is a selective norepinephrine reuptake inhibitor (NRI), not to be confused with selective serotonin and norepinephrine reuptake inhibitors (SNRIs) or selective serotonin reuptake inhibitors (SSRIs), both of which are currently the most prescribed form of antidepressants. This compound is manufactured, marketed and sold in the United States under the brand name Strattera by Eli Lilly and Company as a hydrochloride salt (_____ HCl), the original patent filing company, and current U.S. patent owner.

a. Orphenadrine
b. Aventyl
c. Olopatadine
d. Atomoxetine

5. . _____ is a psychostimulant drug which is known to produce increased wakefulness and focus as well as decreased fatigue and decreased appetite.

_____ is the dextrorotatory, or 'right-handed', stereoisomer of the amphetamine molecule. The amphetamine molecule has two stereoisomers; levoamphetamine and _____.

a. Dextromethorphan
b. Dextroamphetamine
c. Dicloxacillin

1. b
2. b
3. a
4. d
5. b

You can take the complete Online Interactive Chapter Practice Test

for 10. UNIT-10 Central Nervous System Agents,
on all key terms, persons, places, and concepts.

No Additional Costs

http://www.Cram101.com

Register, send an email request to Travis.Reese@Cram101.com to get your user Id and password.

Include your customer order number, and ISBN number from your studyguide Retailer.

CHAPTER OUTLINE: KEY TERMS, PEOPLE, PLACES, CONCEPTS

	Citalopram
	Escitalopram
	Fluoxetine
	Phenelzine
	Dysthymia
	Mechanism of action
	Risk factor
	Serotonin syndrome
	Antidepressants
	Nefazodone
	Trazodone
	Pharmacokinetics
	Clorazepate
	Estazolam
	Eszopiclone
	Triazolam
	Zaleplon
	Zolpidem
	Generalized Anxiety Disorder
	Panic disorder
	Symptoms

	Obsessive-compulsive disorder
	Buspirone
	Clomipramine
	Diazepam
	Insomnia
	Antipsychotic
	Benzisoxazole
	Clozapine
	Fluphenazine
	Mesoridazine
	Phenothiazine
	Trifluoperazine
	Ziprasidone
	Akathisia
	Extrapyramidal symptoms
	Schizophrenia
	Molindone
	Perphenazine
	Acamprosate
	Disulfiram
	Substance abuse

CHAPTER OUTLINE: KEY TERMS, PEOPLE, PLACES, CONCEPTS

	Naloxone
	Naltrexone

CHAPTER HIGHLIGHTS & NOTES: KEY TERMS, PEOPLE, PLACES, CONCEPTS

Citalopram	Citalopram is an antidepressant drug of the selective serotonin reuptake inhibitor (SSRI) class. It has U.S. Food and Drug Administration (FDA) approval to treat major depression, and is prescribed off-label for other conditions. In UK, Germany, Portugal, Poland, and most European countries it is licenced for depressive episodes and panic disorder with or without agoraphobia.
Escitalopram	Escitalopram (trade names Nexito, Anxiset-E (India), Exodus (Brazil), Esto (Israel), Lexapro, Cipralex, Seroplex, Elicea, Lexamil, Lexam, Entact (Greece), Losita (Bangladesh), Reposil (Chile), Animaxen (Colombia), Esitalo (Australia)), Lexamil (South Africa), is an antidepressant of the selective serotonin reuptake inhibitor (SSRI) class. It is approved by the U.S. Food and Drug Administration (FDA) for the treatment of adults and children over 12 years of age with major depressive disorder and generalized anxiety disorder. Escitalopram is the (S)-stereoisomer (enantiomer) of the earlier Lundbeck drug citalopram, hence the name escitalopram.
Fluoxetine	Fluoxetine (also known by the tradenames Prozac, Sarafem, Fontex, among others) is an antidepressant of the selective serotonin reuptake inhibitor (SSRI) class. Fluoxetine was first documented in 1974 by scientists from Eli Lilly and Company. It was presented to the U.S. Food and Drug Administration in February 1977, with Eli Lilly receiving final approval to market the drug in December 1987. Fluoxetine went off-patent in August 2001.
Phenelzine	Phenelzine is a non-selective and irreversible monoamine oxidase inhibitor (MAOI) of the hydrazine class which is used as an antidepressant and anxiolytic. Along with tranylcypromine and isocarboxazid, phenelzine is one of the few non-selective MAOIs still in widespread clinical use. It is typically available in 15 mg tablets and doses usually range from 30-90 mg per day, with 15 mg every day or every other day suggested as a maintenance dose following a successful course of treatment.
Dysthymia	Dysthymia, from Ancient Greek d?s??µ?a, 'melancholy'), also known as neurotic depression, dysthymic disorder, and chronic depression, is a mood disorder consisting of the same cognitive and physical problems as in depression, with less severe but longer-lasting symptoms. The concept was coined by Dr. Robert Spitzer as a replacement for the term 'depressive personality' in the late 1970s.

11. UNIT-11 Psychotropic Agents,

Mechanism of action	In pharmacology, the term mechanism of action refers to the specific biochemical interaction through which a drug substance produces its pharmacological effect. A mechanism of action usually includes mention of the specific molecular targets to which the drug binds, such as an enzyme or receptor. For example, the mechanism of action of aspirin involves irreversible inhibition of the enzyme cyclooxygenase, therefore suppressing the production of prostaglandins and thromboxanes, thereby reducing pain and inflammation.
Risk factor	In epidemiology, a risk factor is a variable associated with an increased risk of disease or infection. Sometimes, determinant is also used, being a variable associated with either increased or decreased risk.
Serotonin syndrome	Serotonin syndrome is a potentially life-threatening adverse drug reaction that may occur following therapeutic drug use, inadvertent interactions between drugs, overdose of particular drugs, or the recreational use of certain drugs. Serotonin syndrome is not an idiosyncratic drug reaction; it is a predictable consequence of excess serotonergic activity at central nervous system (CNS) and peripheral serotonin receptors. For this reason, some experts strongly prefer the terms serotonin toxicity or serotonin toxidrome because these more accurately reflect the fact that it is a form of poisoning.
Antidepressants	Antidepressants are drugs used for the treatment of depression. Despite their name, they are often used to treat a wide range of other conditions, on- or off-label, such as anxiety disorders, obsessive compulsive disorder, eating disorders, chronic pain, neuropathic pain, and some hormone-mediated disorders such as dysmenorrhea, and for snoring, migraines, attention-deficit hyperactivity disorder (ADHD), substance abuse, and occasionally even insomnia or other sleep disorders. They can be used both alone or combination with other medications.
Nefazodone	Nefazodone is an antidepressant marketed by Bristol-Myers Squibb. Its sale was discontinued in 2003 in some countries due to the rare incidence of hepatotoxicity (liver damage), which could lead to the need for a liver transplant, or even death. The incidence of severe liver damage is approximately 1 in every 250,000 to 300,000 patient-years.
Trazodone	Trazodone is an antidepressant of the serotonin antagonist and reuptake inhibitor (SARI) class. It is a phenylpiperazine compound. Trazodone also has anti-anxiety (anxiolytic) and sleep-inducing (hypnotic) effects.
Pharmacokinetics	Pharmacokinetics, is a branch of pharmacology dedicated to the determination of the fate of substances administered externally to a living organism. The substances of interest include pharmaceutical agents, hormones, nutrients, and toxins.

	Pharmacokinetics includes the study of the mechanisms of absorption and distribution of an administered drug, the chemical changes of the substance in the body (e.g. by metabolic enzymes such as CYP or UGT enzymes), and the effects and routes of excretion of the metabolites of the drug.
Clorazepate	Clorazepate (marketed under the brand names Tranxene and Novo-Clopate), also known as clorazepate dipotassium, is a drug that is a benzodiazepine derivative. It possesses anxiolytic, anticonvulsant, sedative, hypnotic and skeletal muscle relaxant properties. Clorazepate is a prodrug for desmethyldiazepam, which is rapidly produced as an active metabolite. Desmethyldiazepam is responsible for most of the therapeutic effects of clorazepate.
Estazolam	Estazolam is a benzodiazepine derivative drug developed by Upjohn in the 1970s. It possesses anxiolytic, anticonvulsant, sedative and skeletal muscle relaxant properties. Estazolam is an intermediate-acting oral benzodiazepine.
Eszopiclone	Eszopiclone, marketed by Sepracor under the brand-name Lunesta, is a nonbenzodiazepine hypnotic used as a treatment for insomnia. Eszopiclone is the active dextrorotatory stereoisomer of zopiclone, and belongs to the class of drugs known as cyclopyrrolones. Eszopiclone is a short acting nonbenzodiazepine sedative hypnotic.
Triazolam	Triazolam is a benzodiazepine drug. It possesses pharmacological properties similar to that of other benzodiazepines, but it is generally only used as a sedative to treat severe insomnia. In addition to the hypnotic properties triazolam possesses, amnesic, anxiolytic, sedative, anticonvulsant and muscle relaxant properties are also present.
Zaleplon	Zaleplon is a sedative-hypnotic, almost entirely used for the management/treatment of insomnia. It is a nonbenzodiazepine hypnotic from the pyrazolopyrimidine class. Sonata (US) is manufactured by King Pharmaceuticals of Bristol, TN. Gedeon Richter Plc.
Zolpidem	Zolpidem (brand names Ambien, Ambien CR, Intermezzo, Stilnox, and Sublinox) is a prescription medication used for the treatment of insomnia and some brain disorders. It is a short-acting nonbenzodiazepine hypnotic of the imidazopyridine class that potentiates GABA, an inhibitory neurotransmitter, by binding to $GABA_A$ receptors at the same location as benzodiazepines. It works quickly, usually within 15 minutes, and has a short half-life of two to three hours.
Generalized Anxiety Disorder	Generalized anxiety disorder is an anxiety disorder that is characterized by excessive, uncontrollable, unexplained and often irrational worry about everyday things that is disproportionate to the actual source of worry. For diagnosis of this disorder, symptoms must last at least six months.

11. UNIT-11 Psychotropic Agents,

Panic disorder	Panic disorder is an anxiety disorder characterized by recurring severe panic attacks. It may also include significant behavioral changes lasting at least a month and of ongoing worry about the implications or concern about having other attacks. The latter are called anticipatory attacks (DSM-IVR).
Symptoms	A symptom is a departure from normal function or feeling which is noticed by a patient, indicating the presence of disease or abnormality. A symptom is subjective, observed by the patient, and cannot be measured directly. The term is sometimes also applied to physiological states outside the context of disease, as for example when referring to 'symptoms of pregnancy'.
Obsessive-compulsive disorder	Obsessive-compulsive disorder is an anxiety disorder characterized by intrusive thoughts that produce uneasiness, apprehension, fear, or worry; by repetitive behaviors aimed at reducing the associated anxiety; or by a combination of such obsessions and compulsions. Symptoms of the disorder include excessive washing or cleaning; repeated checking; extreme hoarding; preoccupation with sexual, violent or religious thoughts; relationship-related obsessions; aversion to particular numbers; and nervous rituals, such as opening and closing a door a certain number of times before entering or leaving a room. These symptoms can be alienating and time-consuming, and often cause severe emotional and financial distress.
Buspirone	Buspirone, trade name Buspar, is an anxiolytic psychoactive drug of the azapirone chemical class and is primarily used to treat generalized anxiety disorder (GAD). In 1986, Bristol-Myers Squibb (BMS) gained Food and Drug Administration (FDA) approval for buspirone in the treatment of GAD. The BMS patent placed on buspirone expired in 2001 and buspirone is now available as a generic drug. Medical uses•Generalized anxiety disorder (GAD) of mild to moderate intensity•Clinical depression augmentation agent alongside drug therapy with an SSRI (selective serotonin reuptake inhibitor) Although not approved for this indication, studies have shown buspirone to be an effective augmentation agent alongside treatment with SSRIs for clinical depression.
Clomipramine	Clomipramine is a tricyclic antidepressant (TCA). It was developed in the 1960s by the Swiss drug manufacturer Geigy (now known as Novartis) and has been in clinical use worldwide ever since.
Diazepam	Diazepam, first marketed as Valium by Hoffmann-La Roche, is a benzodiazepine drug. It is commonly used to treat anxiety, panic attacks, insomnia, seizures, muscle spasms (such as in tetanus cases), restless legs syndrome, alcohol withdrawal, benzodiazepine withdrawal, opiate withdrawal syndrome and Ménière's disease.

11. UNIT-11 Psychotropic Agents,

Insomnia	Insomnia, is a sleep disorder in which there is an inability to fall asleep or to stay asleep as long as desired. While the term is sometimes used to describe a disorder demonstrated by polysomnographic evidence of disturbed sleep, insomnia is often practically defined as a positive response to either of two questions: 'Do you experience difficulty sleeping?' or 'Do you have difficulty falling or staying asleep?' Insomnia is most often thought of as both a sign and a symptom that can accompany several sleep, medical, and psychiatric disorders characterized by a persistent difficulty falling asleep and/or staying asleep or sleep of poor quality. Insomnia is typically followed by functional impairment while awake.
Antipsychotic	An antipsychotic is a psychiatric medication primarily used to manage psychosis (including delusions, hallucinations, or disordered thought), particularly in schizophrenia and bipolar disorder, and is increasingly being used in the management of non-psychotic disorders (ATC code N05A). A first generation of antipsychotics, known as typical antipsychotics, was discovered in the 1950s. Most of the drugs in the second generation, known as atypical antipsychotics, have been developed more recently, although the first atypical antipsychotic, clozapine, was discovered in the 1950s and introduced clinically in the 1970s.
Benzisoxazole	Benzisoxazole is an aromatic organic compound with a molecular formula C_7H_5NO containing a benzene-fused isoxazole ring structure. Benzisoxazole has no household use. It is used primarily in industry and research.
Clozapine	Clozapine is an atypical antipsychotic medication used in the treatment of schizophrenia, and is also sometimes used off-label for the treatment of bipolar disorder. The first of the atypical antipsychotics to be developed, it was first introduced in Europe in 1971, but was voluntarily withdrawn by the manufacturer in 1975 after it was shown to cause agranulocytosis, a condition involving a dangerous decrease in the number of white blood cells, that led to death in some patients. In 1989 after studies demonstrated that it was effective in treating treatment-resistant schizophrenia the United States Food and Drug Administration (FDA) approved the use of clozapine solely for that use, requiring regular white blood cell and absolute neutrophil counts.
Fluphenazine	Fluphenazine is a typical antipsychotic drug used for the treatment of psychoses such as schizophrenia, manic phases of bipolar disorder, agitation, and dementia. It belongs to the piperazine class of phenothiazines. The medication may help control symptoms by blocking or lessening the effects of dopamine in the brain.
Mesoridazine	Mesoridazine is a piperidine neuroleptic drug belonging to the class of drugs called phenothiazines, used in the treatment of schizophrenia. It is a metabolite of thioridazine. The drug's name is derived from the methylsulfoxy and piperidine functional groups in its chemical structure.

11. UNIT-11 Psychotropic Agents,

Phenothiazine	Phenothiazine is an organic compound that occurs in various antipsychotic and antihistaminic drugs. It has the formula $S(C_6H_4)_2NH$. This yellow tricyclic compound is soluble in acetic acid, benzene, and ether. The compound is related to the thiazine-class of heterocyclic compounds.
Trifluoperazine	Trifluoperazine is a typical antipsychotic of the phenothiazine chemical class.
Ziprasidone	Ziprasidone was the fifth atypical antipsychotic to gain approval (February 2001) in the United States. It is approved by the U.S. Food and Drug Administration (FDA) for the treatment of schizophrenia, and acute mania and mixed states associated with bipolar disorder. Its intramuscular injection form is approved for acute agitation in schizophrenic patients for whom treatment with just ziprasidone is appropriate.
Akathisia	Akathisia, or acathisia is a syndrome characterized by unpleasant sensations of inner restlessness that manifests itself with an inability to sit still or remain motionless. The term was coined by the Czech neuropsychiatrist Ladislav Haskovec (1866-1944), who described the phenomenon in 1901. Antipsychotics (also known as neuroleptics) may cause akathisia.
Extrapyramidal symptoms	The extrapyramidal system can be affected in a number of ways, which are revealed in a range of extrapyramidal symptoms also known as extrapyramidal side-effects (EPSE), such as akinesia (inability to initiate movement) and akathisia (inability to remain motionless). Extrapyramidal symptoms are various movement disorders such as acute dystonic reactions, pseudoparkinsonism, or akathisia suffered as a result of taking dopamine antagonists, usually antipsychotic (neuroleptic) drugs, which are often used to control psychosis. It can also be a symptom of a metabolic disease.
Schizophrenia	Schizophrenia is a mental disorder characterized by a breakdown of thought processes and by a deficit of typical emotional responses. Common symptoms are delusions and disorganized thinking including auditory hallucinations, paranoia, bizarre delusions, disorganized speech, and it is accompanied by significant social or occupational dysfunction. The onset of symptoms typically occurs in young adulthood, with a global lifetime prevalence of about 0.3-0.7%.
Molindone	Molindone is a therapeutic antipsychotic, used in the treatment of schizophrenia. It works by blocking the effects of dopamine in the brain, leading to diminished psychoses. It is rapidly absorbed when taken by mouth.
Perphenazine	Perphenazine is a typical antipsychotic drug. Chemically, it is classified as a piperazinyl phenothiazine. Originally marketed in the US as Trilafon, it has been in clinical use for decades.
Acamprosate	Acamprosate, also known as N-acetyl homotaurine and by the brand name Campral, is a drug used for treating alcohol and benzodiazepine dependence.

	Acamprosate is thought to stabilize the chemical balance in the brain that would otherwise be disrupted by alcohol withdrawal or benzodiazepine withdrawal, possibly by antagonizing glutaminergic N-methyl--aspartate receptors and agonizing gamma-aminobutyric acid (GABA) type A receptors. Reports indicate that acamprosate works only with a combination of attending support groups and abstinence from alcohol.
Disulfiram	Disulfiram is a drug discovered in the 1920s and used to support the treatment of chronic alcoholism by producing an acute sensitivity to alcohol. Trade names for disulfiram in different countries are Antabuse and Antabus manufactured by Odyssey Pharmaceuticals. Disulfiram is also being studied as a treatment for cocaine dependence, as it prevents the breakdown of dopamine (a neurotransmitter whose release is stimulated by cocaine); the excess dopamine results in increased anxiety, higher blood pressure, restlessness and other unpleasant symptoms.
Substance abuse	Substance abuse, is a patterned use of a substance (drug) in which the user consumes the substance in amounts or with methods neither approved nor advised by medical professionals. Substance abuse/drug abuse is not limited to mood-altering or psycho-active drugs. If an activity is performed using the objects against the rules and policies of the matter (as in steroids for performance enhancement in sports), it is also called substance abuse.
Naloxone	Naloxone is an opioid antagonist drug developed by Sankyo in the 1960s. Naloxone is a drug used to counter the effects of opiate overdose, for example heroin or morphine overdose. Naloxone is specifically used to counteract life-threatening depression of the central nervous system and respiratory system.
Naltrexone	Naltrexone is an opioid receptor antagonist used primarily in the management of alcohol dependence and opioid dependence. It is marketed in generic form as its hydrochloride salt, naltrexone hydrochloride, and marketed under the trade names Revia and Depade. In some countries including the United States, a once-monthly extended-release injectable formulation is marketed under the trade name Vivitrol.

11. UNIT-11 Psychotropic Agents,

1. _____ (also known by the tradenames Prozac, Sarafem, Fontex, among others) is an antidepressant of the selective serotonin reuptake inhibitor (SSRI) class. _____ was first documented in 1974 by scientists from Eli Lilly and Company. It was presented to the U.S. Food and Drug Administration in February 1977, with Eli Lilly receiving final approval to market the drug in December 1987. _____ went off-patent in August 2001.

   a. Methamphetamine
   b. Homeopathic
   c. Chiropractic
   d. Fluoxetine

2. _____ is an antidepressant drug of the selective serotonin reuptake inhibitor (SSRI) class. It has U.S. Food and Drug Administration (FDA) approval to treat major depression, and is prescribed off-label for other conditions. In UK, Germany, Portugal, Poland, and most European countries it is licenced for depressive episodes and panic disorder with or without agoraphobia.

   a. Venlafaxine
   b. Celexa
   c. Citalopram
   d. Prozac

3. _____ (trade names Nexito, Anxiset-E (India), Exodus (Brazil), Esto (Israel), Lexapro, Cipralex, Seroplex, Elicea, Lexamil, Lexam, Entact (Greece), Losita (Bangladesh), Reposil (Chile), Animaxen (Colombia), Esitalo (Australia)), Lexamil (South Africa), is an antidepressant of the selective serotonin reuptake inhibitor (SSRI) class. It is approved by the U.S. Food and Drug Administration (FDA) for the treatment of adults and children over 12 years of age with major depressive disorder and generalized anxiety disorder. _____ is the (S)-stereoisomer (enantiomer) of the earlier Lundbeck drug citalopram, hence the name _____.

   a. Prozac
   b. Escitalopram
   c. isomer
   d. Prozac

4. . The extrapyramidal system can be affected in a number of ways, which are revealed in a range of _____ also known as extrapyramidal side-effects (EPSE), such as akinesia (inability to initiate movement) and akathisia (inability to remain motionless).

   _____ are various movement disorders such as acute dystonic reactions, pseudoparkinsonism, or akathisia suffered as a result of taking dopamine antagonists, usually antipsychotic (neuroleptic) drugs, which are often used to control psychosis. It can also be a symptom of a metabolic disease.

   a. Homeopathic
   b. Bendroflumethiazide
   c. Extrapyramidal symptoms

5. _____ is a non-selective and irreversible monoamine oxidase inhibitor (MAOI) of the hydrazine class which is used as an antidepressant and anxiolytic. Along with tranylcypromine and isocarboxazid, _____ is one of the few non-selective MAOIs still in widespread clinical use. It is typically available in 15 mg tablets and doses usually range from 30-90 mg per day, with 15 mg every day or every other day suggested as a maintenance dose following a successful course of treatment.

a. Pheniprazine
b. Phenelzine
c. Phenylhydrazine
d. Piperine

1. d
2. c
3. b
4. c
5. b

You can take the complete Online Interactive Chapter Practice Test

for 11. UNIT-11 Psychotropic Agents,
on all key terms, persons, places, and concepts.

No Additional Costs

http://www.Cram101.com

Register, send an email request to Travis.Reese@Cram101.com to get your user Id and password.

Include your customer order number, and ISBN number from your studyguide Retailer.

12. UNIT-12 Endocrine Agents,

CHAPTER OUTLINE: KEY TERMS, PEOPLE, PLACES, CONCEPTS

	Adrenal cortex
	Aldosterone
	Cortisol
	Cortisone
	Glucocorticoid
	Pharmacokinetics
	Dexamethasone
	Liothyronine
	Liotrix
	Methimazole
	Propylthiouracil
	Thyroid gland
	Thyrotropin
	Triiodothyronine
	Hyperthyroidism
	Mechanism of action
	Exenatide
	Metformin
	Miglitol
	Pioglitazone
	Pramlintide

	Repaglinide
	Rosiglitazone
	Gluconeogenesis
	Islets of Langerhans
	Secretion
	Amylin
	Dopamine agonist
	Combination

CHAPTER HIGHLIGHTS & NOTES: KEY TERMS, PEOPLE, PLACES, CONCEPTS

Adrenal cortex	Situated along the perimeter of the adrenal gland, the adrenal cortex mediates the stress response through the production of mineralocorticoids and glucocorticoids, including aldosterone and cortisol respectively. It is also a secondary site of androgen synthesis. Recent data suggest that adrenocortical cells under pathological as well as under physiological conditions show neuroendocrine properties; within the normal adrenal, this neuroendocrine differentiation seems to be restricted to cells of the zona glomerulosa and might be important for an autocrine regulation of adrenocortical function.
Aldosterone	Aldosterone is a steroid hormone (mineralocorticoid family) produced by the outer section (zona glomerulosa) of the adrenal cortex in the adrenal gland. It acts mainly on the distal tubules and collecting ducts of the nephron, the functional unit of the kidney, to cause the conservation of sodium, secretion of potassium, increased water retention, and increased blood pressure. The overall effect of aldosterone is to increase reabsorption of ions and water in the kidney -- increasing blood volume and, therefore, increasing blood pressure.
Cortisol	Cortisol, known more formally as hydrocortisone is a steroid hormone, more specifically a glucocorticoid, produced by the zona fasciculata of the adrenal cortex. It is released in response to stress and a low level of blood glucocorticoids.

Cortisone	Cortisone is a 21-carbon steroid hormone. It is one of the main hormones released by the adrenal gland in response to stress. In chemical structure, it is a corticosteroid closely related to corticosterone. It is used to treat a variety of ailments and can be administered intravenously, orally, intraarticularly (into a joint), or transcutaneously. Cortisone suppresses the immune system, thus reducing inflammation and attendant pain and swelling at the site of the injury. Risks exist, in particular in the long-term use of cortisone.
Glucocorticoid	Glucocorticoids (GC) are a class of steroid hormones that bind to the glucocorticoid receptor (GR), which is present in almost every vertebrate animal cell. The name glucocorticoid derives from its role in the regulation of the metabolism of glucose, its synthesis in the adrenal cortex, and its steroidal structure .
	GCs are part of the feedback mechanism in the immune system that turns immune activity (inflammation) down.
Pharmacokinetics	Pharmacokinetics, is a branch of pharmacology dedicated to the determination of the fate of substances administered externally to a living organism. The substances of interest include pharmaceutical agents, hormones, nutrients, and toxins.
	Pharmacokinetics includes the study of the mechanisms of absorption and distribution of an administered drug, the chemical changes of the substance in the body (e.g. by metabolic enzymes such as CYP or UGT enzymes), and the effects and routes of excretion of the metabolites of the drug.
Dexamethasone	Dexamethasone is a potent synthetic member of the glucocorticoid class of steroid drugs. It acts as an anti-inflammatory and immunosuppressant. When taken orally, it is 26.6 times more potent than the naturally occurring hormone cortisol and 6.6 times more potent than prednisone.
Liothyronine	Liothyronine is a form of thyroid hormone used to treat hypothyroidism and myxedema coma. It is marketed as the sodium salt under the brand name Cytomel (or Tertroxin in Australia).
Liotrix	Liotrix is 4:1 mixture of thyroxine and triiodothyronine (T_3) made synthetically. It is used to replenish thyroid hormones in thyroid deficiency and hypothyroidism. The only brand of liotrix available in the U.S. is Thyrolar, manufactured by Forest Laboratories.
Methimazole	Methimazole is an antithyroid drug, and part of the thioamide group. Like its counterpart propylthiouracil, a major side effect of treatment is agranulocytosis.
Propylthiouracil	Propylthiouracil or 6-n-propylthiouracil is a thiouracil-derived drug used to treat hyperthyroidism (including Graves' disease) by decreasing the amount of thyroid hormone produced by the thyroid gland. Its notable side effects include a risk of agranulocytosis and aplastic anemia.

12. UNIT-12 Endocrine Agents,

Thyroid gland	The thyroid gland or simply, the thyroid, in vertebrate anatomy, is one of the largest endocrine glands and consists of two connected lobes. The thyroid gland is found in the neck, below the thyroid cartilage (which forms the laryngeal prominence, or 'Adam's apple'). The thyroid gland controls how quickly the body uses energy, makes proteins, and controls how sensitive the body is to other hormones.
Thyrotropin	Thyroid-stimulating hormone (also known as TSH or thyrotropin) is a hormone that stimulates the thyroid gland to produce thyroxine, and then triiodothyronine (T_3) which stimulates the metabolism of almost every tissue in the body. It is a glycoprotein hormone synthesized and secreted by thyrotrope cells in the anterior pituitary gland, which regulates the endocrine function of the thyroid gland.
Triiodothyronine	Triiodothyronine, is a thyroid hormone. It affects almost every physiological process in the body, including growth and development, metabolism, body temperature, and heart rate. Production of T_3 and its prohormone thyroxine (T_4) is activated by thyroid-stimulating hormone (TSH), which is released from the pituitary gland.
Hyperthyroidism	Hyperthyroidism, is a condition in which the thyroid gland produces and secretes excessive amounts of the free thyroid hormones, triiodothyronine (T3) and/or thyroxine (T4). This is the opposite of hypothyroidism ('sluggish thyroid'), which is the reduced production and secretion of T3 and/or T4. Hyperthyroidism is a type of thyrotoxicosis, a hypermetabolic clinical syndrome which occurs when there are elevated serum levels of T3 and/or T4. Graves' disease is the most common cause of hyperthyroidism. While hyperthyroidism may cause thyrotoxicosis they are not synonymous medical conditions; some patients may develop thyrotoxicosis as a result of inflammation of the thyroid gland (thyroiditis), which may cause the release of excessive thyroid hormone already stored in the gland but does not cause accelerated hormone production.
Mechanism of action	In pharmacology, the term mechanism of action refers to the specific biochemical interaction through which a drug substance produces its pharmacological effect. A mechanism of action usually includes mention of the specific molecular targets to which the drug binds, such as an enzyme or receptor. For example, the mechanism of action of aspirin involves irreversible inhibition of the enzyme cyclooxygenase, therefore suppressing the production of prostaglandins and thromboxanes, thereby reducing pain and inflammation.
Exenatide	Exenatide is a glucagon-like peptide-1 agonist (GLP-1 agonist) medication, belonging to the group of incretin mimetics, approved in April 2005 for the treatment of diabetes mellitus type 2.

	Exenatide in its Byetta form is administered as a subcutaneous injection (under the skin) of the abdomen, thigh, or arm, any time within the 60 minutes before the first and last meal of the day. A once-weekly injection has been approved as of January 27, 2012 under the trademark Bydureon. It is manufactured by Amylin Pharmaceuticals and commercialized by Astrazeneca.
Metformin	Metformin is an oral antidiabetic drug in the biguanide class. It is the first-line drug of choice for the treatment of type 2 diabetes, in particular, in overweight and obese people and those with normal kidney function. Its use in gestational diabetes has been limited by safety concerns.
Miglitol	Miglitol is an oral anti-diabetic drug that acts by inhibiting the ability of the patient to break down complex carbohydrates into glucose. It is primarily used in diabetes mellitus type 2 for establishing greater glycemic control by preventing the digestion of carbohydrates (such as disaccharides, oligosaccharides, and polysaccharides) into monosaccharides which can be absorbed by the body. Miglitol inhibits glycoside hydrolase enzymes called alpha-glucosidases.
Pioglitazone	Pioglitazone is a prescription drug of the class thiazolidinedione (TZD) with hypoglycemic (antihyperglycemic, antidiabetic) action to treat diabetes. It is used to improve glucose control in adults over the age of 18 with type 2 diabetes. Pioglitazone is marketed as trademarks Actos in the USA, Canada, the UK and Germany, Glustin in Europe, Glizone and Pioz in India by Zydus Cadila and USV Limited, respectively and Zactos in Mexico by Takeda Pharmaceuticals.
Pramlintide	Pramlintide is a relatively new injectable drug for diabetes (both type 1 and 2), developed by Amylin Pharmaceuticals (now a wholly owned subsidiary of AstraZeneca). Pramlintide is sold as an acetate salt.
Repaglinide	Repaglinide is an antidiabetic drug in the class of medications known as meglitinides, and was invented in 1983. It is sold by Novo Nordisk under the name of Prandin in the U.S., GlucoNorm in Canada, Surepost in Japan, Repaglinide in Egypt by EIPICO, and NovoNorm elsewhere. In Japan it is produced by Dainippon Sumitomo Pharma.
Rosiglitazone	Rosiglitazone (trade name Avandia, GlaxoSmithKline) is an antidiabetic drug in the thiazolidinedione class of drugs. It works as an insulin sensitizer, by binding to the PPAR receptors in fat cells and making the cells more responsive to insulin. It is marketed by the pharmaceutical company GlaxoSmithKline (GSK) as a stand-alone drug or in combination with metformin (trade name Avandamet) or with glimepiride (trade name Avandaryl).
Gluconeogenesis	Gluconeogenesis is a metabolic pathway that results in the generation of glucose from non-carbohydrate carbon substrates such as lactate, glycerol, and glucogenic amino acids. It is one of the two main mechanisms humans and many other animals use to keep blood glucose levels from dropping too low (hypoglycemia).

12. UNIT-12 Endocrine Agents,

Islets of Langerhans	The islets of Langerhans are the regions of the pancreas that contain its endocrine cells. Discovered in 1869 by German pathological anatomist Paul Langerhans at the age of 22, the islets of Langerhans constitute approximately 1% to 2% of the mass of the pancreas.
Secretion	Secretion is the process of elaborating, releasing, and oozing chemicals, or a secreted chemical substance from a cell or gland. In contrast to excretion, the substance may have a certain function, rather than being a waste product. Many cells contain this such as glucoma cells.
Amylin	Amylin, or Islet Amyloid Polypeptide, is a 37-residue peptide hormone. It is cosecreted with insulin from the pancreatic ß-cells in the ratio of approximately 100:1. Amylin plays a role in glycemic regulation by slowing gastric emptying and promoting satiety, thereby preventing post-prandial spikes in blood glucose levels. IAPP is processed from an 89-residue coding sequence.
Dopamine agonist	A dopamine agonist is a compound that activates dopamine receptors in the absence of dopamine. Dopamine agonists activate signaling pathways through the dopamine receptor and trimeric G-proteins, ultimately leading to changes in gene transcription.
Combination	In mathematics, a combination is a way of selecting members from a grouping, such that the order of selection does not matter. In smaller cases it is possible to count the number of combinations. For example given three fruits, say an apple, an orange and a pear, there are three combinations of two that can be drawn from this set: an apple and a pear; an apple and an orange; or a pear and an orange.

1. Situated along the perimeter of the adrenal gland, the _____ mediates the stress response through the production of mineralocorticoids and glucocorticoids, including aldosterone and cortisol respectively. It is also a secondary site of androgen synthesis. Recent data suggest that adrenocortical cells under pathological as well as under physiological conditions show neuroendocrine properties; within the normal adrenal, this neuroendocrine differentiation seems to be restricted to cells of the zona glomerulosa and might be important for an autocrine regulation of adrenocortical function.

   a. Adrenal cortex
   b. Orphan Drug Act
   c. Esomeprazole
   d. Epristeride

2. . _____ is a steroid hormone (mineralocorticoid family) produced by the outer section (zona glomerulosa) of the adrenal cortex in the adrenal gland.

It acts mainly on the distal tubules and collecting ducts of the nephron, the functional unit of the kidney, to cause the conservation of sodium, secretion of potassium, increased water retention, and increased blood pressure. The overall effect of _____ is to increase reabsorption of ions and water in the kidney -- increasing blood volume and, therefore, increasing blood pressure.

a. isomer
b. Orphan Drug Act
c. Esomeprazole
d. Aldosterone

3. _____, known more formally as hydrocortisone is a steroid hormone, more specifically a glucocorticoid, produced by the zona fasciculata of the adrenal cortex. It is released in response to stress and a low level of blood glucocorticoids. Its primary functions are to increase blood sugar through gluconeogenesis; suppress the immune system; and aid in fat, protein and carbohydrate metabolism.

a. Kanamycin sulfate
b. Penicillin G
c. Cortisol
d. Benzylpenicillin

4. _____ is an oral antidiabetic drug in the biguanide class. It is the first-line drug of choice for the treatment of type 2 diabetes, in particular, in overweight and obese people and those with normal kidney function. Its use in gestational diabetes has been limited by safety concerns.

a. Methyldopa
b. Methylene blue
c. Metoclopramide
d. Metformin

5. _____ is an oral anti-diabetic drug that acts by inhibiting the ability of the patient to break down complex carbohydrates into glucose. It is primarily used in diabetes mellitus type 2 for establishing greater glycemic control by preventing the digestion of carbohydrates (such as disaccharides, oligosaccharides, and polysaccharides) into monosaccharides which can be absorbed by the body.

_____ inhibits glycoside hydrolase enzymes called alpha-glucosidases.

a. Humalog
b. Pancrelipase
c. Miglitol
d. Clidinium

1. a
2. d
3. c
4. d
5. c

You can take the complete Online Interactive Chapter Practice Test

for 12. UNIT-12 Endocrine Agents,
on all key terms, persons, places, and concepts.

No Additional Costs

http://www.Cram101.com

Register, send an email request to Travis.Reese@Cram101.com to get your user Id and password.

Include your customer order number, and ISBN number from your studyguide Retailer.

13. UNIT-13 Reproductive System Medications,

_____ | Levonorgestrel

_____ | Follicle-stimulating hormone

_____ | Gonadotropin-releasing hormone

_____ | Menstrual cycle

_____ | Progesterone

_____ | Estradiol

_____ | Ethinyl estradiol

_____ | Mechanism of action

_____ | Transdermal

_____ | Intrauterine device

_____ | Drospirenone

_____ | Pharmacokinetics

_____ | Estriol

_____ | Estrone

_____ | Methyltestosterone

_____ | Hormone replacement therapy

_____ | Androgen

_____ | Estropipate

_____ | Hypogonadism

_____ | Anastrozole

_____ | Antiestrogen

	Aromatase inhibitors
	Breast cancer
	Exemestane
	Tamoxifen
	Toremifene
	Metastatic
	Risk factor

Levonorgestrel	Levonorgestrel is a second generation synthetic progestogen used as an active ingredient in some hormonal contraceptives, including combined oral contraceptive pills, progestogen only pills, emergency contraceptive pills, intrauterine systems, contraceptive implants, and hormone replacement therapy.
Follicle-stimulating hormone	Follicle-stimulating hormone is a hormone found in humans and other animals. It is synthesized and secreted by gonadotrophs of the anterior pituitary gland. Follicle stimulating hormone regulates the development, growth, pubertal maturation, and reproductive processes of the body.
Gonadotropin-releasing hormone	Gonadotropin-releasing hormone also known as Luteinizing-hormone-releasing hormone (LHRH) and luliberin, is a trophic peptide hormone responsible for the release of follicle-stimulating hormone (FSH) and luteinizing hormone (LH) from the anterior pituitary. GnRH is synthesized and released from neurons within the hypothalamus. The peptide belongs to gonadotropin-releasing hormone family.
Menstrual cycle	The menstrual cycle is the scientific term for the physiological changes that occur in fertile women and other female primates for the purposes of sexual reproduction. The menstrual cycle, under the control of the endocrine system, is necessary for reproduction. It is commonly divided into three phases: the follicular phase, ovulation, and the luteal phase.

13. UNIT-13 Reproductive System Medications,

Progesterone	Progesterone also known as P4 is a C-21 steroid hormone involved in the female menstrual cycle, pregnancy (supports gestation) and embryogenesis of humans and other species. Progesterone belongs to a class of hormones called progestogens, and is the major naturally occurring human progestogen.
Estradiol	Estradiol is a sex hormone. Estradiol is abbreviated E2 as it has two hydroxyl groups in its molecular structure. Estrone has one (E1) and estriol has three (E3). Estradiol is about 10 times as potent as estrone and about 80 times as potent as estriol in its estrogenic effect. Except during the early follicular phase of the menstrual cycle, its serum levels are somewhat higher than that of estrone during the reproductive years of the human female. Thus it is the predominant estrogen during reproductive years both in terms of absolute serum levels as well as in terms of estrogenic activity.
Ethinyl estradiol	Ethinyl estradiol also ethynyl estradiol, or ethinyl oestradiol, is a derivative of 17β-estradiol (E2), the major endogenous estrogen in humans. EE is an orally bioactive estrogen used in many formulations of combined oral contraceptive pills. It is one of the most commonly used medications for this purpose.
Mechanism of action	In pharmacology, the term mechanism of action refers to the specific biochemical interaction through which a drug substance produces its pharmacological effect. A mechanism of action usually includes mention of the specific molecular targets to which the drug binds, such as an enzyme or receptor. For example, the mechanism of action of aspirin involves irreversible inhibition of the enzyme cyclooxygenase, therefore suppressing the production of prostaglandins and thromboxanes, thereby reducing pain and inflammation.
Transdermal	Transdermal is a route of administration wherein active ingredients are delivered across the skin for systemic distribution. Examples include transdermal patches used for medicine delivery, and transdermal implants used for medical or aesthetic purposes.
Intrauterine device	An intrauterine device is a small contraceptive device, often 'T'-shaped, often containing either copper or levonorgestrel, which is inserted into the uterus. They are one form of long-acting reversible contraception which are the most effective types of reversible birth control. Failure rates with the copper IUD is about 0.8% while the levonorgestrel IUD has a failure rate of 0.2% in the first year of use.
Drospirenone	Drospirenone, also known as 1,2-dihydrospirorenone, is a synthetic hormone used in birth control pills. It is sold under the brand names Yasmin, Yasminelle, Yaz, Beyaz, Ocella, Zarah, and Angeliq, all of which are combination products of drospirenone with an estrogen such as ethinylestradiol.

Pharmacokinetics	Pharmacokinetics, is a branch of pharmacology dedicated to the determination of the fate of substances administered externally to a living organism. The substances of interest include pharmaceutical agents, hormones, nutrients, and toxins. Pharmacokinetics includes the study of the mechanisms of absorption and distribution of an administered drug, the chemical changes of the substance in the body (e.g. by metabolic enzymes such as CYP or UGT enzymes), and the effects and routes of excretion of the metabolites of the drug.
Estriol	Estriol is one of the three main estrogens produced by the human body.
Estrone	Estrone is an estrogenic hormone secreted by the ovary as well as adipose tissue with the chemical name of 3-hydroxyestra-1,3,5(10)-triene-17-one and athechemical formula $C_{18}H_{22}O_2$. Estrone is an odorless, solid crystalline powder, white in color with a melting point of 254.5 °C and a specific gravity of 1.23. Estrone is one of several natural estrogens, which also include estriol and estradiol. Estrone is the least abundant of the three hormones; estradiol is present almost always in the reproductive female body, and estriol is abundant primarily during pregnancy.
Methyltestosterone	Methyltestosterone is a 17-alpha-alkylated anabolic steroid used to treat men with a testosterone deficiency. It bears close structural similarity to testosterone, but has a methyl group at C17 in order to increase oral bioavailability.
Hormone replacement therapy	Hormone replacement therapy refers to any form of hormone therapy wherein the patient, in the course of medical treatment, receives hormones, either to supplement a lack of naturally occurring hormones, or to substitute other hormones for naturally occurring hormones. Common forms of hormone replacement therapy include:•Hormone replacement therapy for menopause is based on the idea that the treatment may prevent discomfort caused by diminished circulating estrogen and progesterone hormones, or in the case of the surgically or prematurely menopausal, that it may prolong life and may reduce incidence of dementia. It involves the use of one or more of a group of medications designed to artificially boost hormone levels.
Androgen	Androgen, also called androgenic hormone or testoid, is the generic term for any natural or synthetic compound, usually a steroid hormone, that stimulates or controls the development and maintenance of male characteristics in vertebrates by binding to androgen receptors. This includes the activity of the accessory male sex organs and development of male secondary sex characteristics. Androgens were first discovered in 1936. Androgens are also the original anabolic steroids and the precursor of all estrogens, which are stress hormones.
Estropipate	Estropipate is a form of estrogen sold under the brand names Ogen and Ortho-Est. It is a salt of estrone sulfate and piperazine.

13. UNIT-13 Reproductive System Medications,

Hypogonadism	Hypogonadism is a medical term which describes a diminished functional activity of the gonads - the testes and ovaries in males and females, respectively - that may result in diminished sex hormone biosynthesis. In layman's terms, it is sometimes called 'interrupted stage 1 puberty'. Low androgen (e.g., testosterone) levels are referred to as hypoandrogenism and low estrogen (e.g., estradiol) as hypoestrogenism, and may occur as symptoms of hypogonadism in both sexes, but are generally only diagnosed in males and females respectively.
Anastrozole	Anastrozole (marketed under the trade name Arimidex by AstraZeneca) is an aromatase-inhibiting drug approved for treatment of breast cancer after surgery, as well as for metastasis in both pre and post-menopausal women. The severity of breast cancer is increased by estrogen, as sex hormones cause hyperplasia, and differentiation at estrogen receptor sites. Anastrozole works by inhibiting the synthesis of estrogen.
Antiestrogen	An antiestrogen is a substance that blocks the production or utilization of estrogens, or inhibits their effects. (Estrogens are the family of hormones that promote the development and maintenance of female sex characteristics).

Antiestrogens like tamoxifen can promote an invasive phenotype in estrogen receptor (ER)-positive breast cancer cells with deficient intercellular adhesion. |
| Aromatase inhibitors | Aromatase inhibitors are a class of drugs used in the treatment of breast cancer and ovarian cancer in postmenopausal women. AIs may also be used off-label to treat or prevent gynaecomastia in men.

Aromatase is the enzyme that synthesizes estrogen. As breast and ovarian cancers require estrogen to grow, AIs are taken to either block the production of estrogen or block the action of estrogen on receptors. |
Breast cancer	Breast cancer is the development of cancer from breast tissue. Signs of breast cancer may include a lump in the breast, a change in breast shape, dimpling of the skin, fluid coming from the nipple, or a red scaly patch of skin. In those with distant spread of the disease, there may be bone pain, swollen lymph nodes, shortness of breath, or yellow skin.
Exemestane	Exemestane (trade name Aromasin) is a drug used to treat breast cancer. It is a member of the class of drugs known as aromatase inhibitors. Some breast cancers require estrogen to grow. Those cancers have estrogen receptors (ERs), and are called ER-positive. They may also be called estrogen-responsive, hormonally-responsive, or hormone-receptor-positive. Aromatase is an enzyme that synthesizes estrogen. Aromatase inhibitors block the synthesis of estrogen. This lowers the estrogen level, and slows the growth of cancers.
Tamoxifen	Tamoxifen is an antagonist of the estrogen receptor in breast tissue via its active metabolite, hydroxytamoxifen.

	In other tissues such as the endometrium, it behaves as an agonist, and thus may be characterized as a mixed agonist/antagonist. Tamoxifen is the usual endocrine (anti-estrogen) therapy for hormone receptor-positive breast cancer in pre-menopausal women, and is also a standard in post-menopausal women although aromatase inhibitors are also frequently used in that setting.
Toremifene	Toremifene citrate is an oral selective estrogen receptor modulator (SERM) which helps oppose the actions of estrogen in the body. Licensed in the United States under the brand name Fareston, toremifene citrate is FDA-approved for use in advanced (metastatic) breast cancer. It is also being evaluated for prevention of prostate cancer under the brand name Acapodene.
Metastatic	Metastatic disease is the spread of a cancer from one organ or part to another non-adjacent organ or part. The new occurrences of disease thus generated are referred to as metastases It was previously thought that only malignant tumor cells and infections have the capacity to metastasize; however, this is being reconsidered due to new research. In origin metastasis is a Greek word meaning 'displacement', from μετ?, meta, 'next', and στ?σις, stasis, 'placement'.
Risk factor	In epidemiology, a risk factor is a variable associated with an increased risk of disease or infection. Sometimes, determinant is also used, being a variable associated with either increased or decreased risk.

CHAPTER QUIZ: KEY TERMS, PEOPLE, PLACES, CONCEPTS

1. In epidemiology, a _____ is a variable associated with an increased risk of disease or infection. Sometimes, determinant is also used, being a variable associated with either increased or decreased risk.

   a. Homeopathic
   b. Neoplasm
   c. malignant
   d. Risk factor

2. . _____ are a class of drugs used in the treatment of breast cancer and ovarian cancer in postmenopausal women. AIs may also be used off-label to treat or prevent gynaecomastia in men.

   Aromatase is the enzyme that synthesizes estrogen. As breast and ovarian cancers require estrogen to grow, AIs are taken to either block the production of estrogen or block the action of estrogen on receptors.

   a. Homeopathic
   b. Interleukin 2
   c. isomer

3. _____ also known as Luteinizing-hormone-releasing hormone (LHRH) and luliberin, is a trophic peptide hormone responsible for the release of follicle-stimulating hormone (FSH) and luteinizing hormone (LH) from the anterior pituitary. GnRH is synthesized and released from neurons within the hypothalamus. The peptide belongs to _____ family.

   a. Granulocyte colony-stimulating factor
   b. Gonadotropin-releasing hormone
   c. Leptin
   d. Little gastrin I

4. _____ is a second generation synthetic progestogen used as an active ingredient in some hormonal contraceptives, including combined oral contraceptive pills, progestogen only pills, emergency contraceptive pills, intrauterine systems, contraceptive implants, and hormone replacement therapy.

   a. Levopropylhexedrine
   b. Levorphanol
   c. Levonorgestrel
   d. Levosulpiride

5. In pharmacology, the term _____ refers to the specific biochemical interaction through which a drug substance produces its pharmacological effect. A _____ usually includes mention of the specific molecular targets to which the drug binds, such as an enzyme or receptor.

   For example, the _____ of aspirin involves irreversible inhibition of the enzyme cyclooxygenase, therefore suppressing the production of prostaglandins and thromboxanes, thereby reducing pain and inflammation.

   a. Medicinal chemistry
   b. Mechanism of action
   c. Molecular oncology
   d. Negative allosteric modulator

ANSWER KEY
13. UNIT-13 Reproductive System Medications,

1. d
2. d
3. b
4. c
5. b

You can take the complete Online Interactive Chapter Practice Test

for 13. UNIT-13 Reproductive System Medications,
on all key terms, persons, places, and concepts.

No Additional Costs

http://www.Cram101.com

Register, send an email request to Travis.Reese@Cram101.com to get your user Id and password.

Include your customer order number, and ISBN number from your studyguide Retailer.

14. UNIT-14 Antiinfectives,

CHAPTER OUTLINE: KEY TERMS, PEOPLE, PLACES, CONCEPTS

	Fluconazole
	Fosfomycin
	Terconazole
	Tioconazole
	Vancomycin
	Infection
	Antimicrobial
	Cefuroxime
	Chancroid
	Dicloxacillin
	Erythromycin
	Gonorrhea
	Penicillin
	Rocky Mountain spotted fever
	Peptic ulcer disease
	Central nervous system
	Nafcillin
	Oxacillin
	Penicillin G
	Piperacillin
	Ticarcillin

14. UNIT-14 Antiinfectives,

Mechanism of action

Cefdinir

Ceftibuten

Allergy

Cephalexin

Doxycycline

Pharmacokinetics

Tetracycline

Fidaxomicin

Macrolide

Telithromycin

Norfloxacin

Kanamycin

Sulfamethoxazole

Sulfisoxazole

Ethambutol

Risk factor

Tuberculosis treatment

Pyrazinamide

Rifabutin

Rifampicin

14. UNIT-14 Antiinfectives,

CHAPTER OUTLINE: KEY TERMS, PEOPLE, PLACES, CONCEPTS

- Rifapentine
- Capreomycin
- Cycloserine
- Ethionamide
- Anidulafungin
- Azole
- Griseofulvin
- Fungal
- Topical
- Antiretroviral
- Atazanavir
- Darunavir
- Delavirdine
- Enfuvirtide
- Indinavir
- Lamivudine
- Nevirapine
- Protease inhibitor
- Raltegravir
- Stavudine
- Zidovudine

	Oseltamivir
	Rimantadine
	Tinidazole
	Zanamivir
	Herpes simplex
	Malaria
	Chloroquine

CHAPTER HIGHLIGHTS & NOTES: KEY TERMS, PEOPLE, PLACES, CONCEPTS

Fluconazole	Fluconazole is a triazole antifungal drug used in the treatment and prevention of superficial and systemic fungal infections. In a bulk powder form, it appears as a white crystalline powder, and it is very slightly soluble in water and soluble in alcohol. It is commonly marketed under the trade name Diflucan or Trican (Pfizer).
Fosfomycin	Fosfomycin is a broad-spectrum antibiotic produced by certain Streptomyces species. Fosfomycin is not recommended for children and 75 up of age. It can now be made by chemical synthesis.
Terconazole	Terconazole is an anti-fungal medication, primarily used to treat vaginal fungal infections.
Tioconazole	Tioconazole is an antifungal medication of the imidazole class used to treat infections caused by a fungus or yeast. It is marketed under the brand names Trosyd and Gyno-Trosyd (Pfizer). Tioconazole ointments serve to treat women's vaginal yeast infections.
Vancomycin	Vancomycin INN is a glycopeptide antibiotic used in the prophylaxis and treatment of infections caused by Gram-positive bacteria. Vancomycin was first isolated in 1953 at Eli Lilly, from a soil sample collected from the interior jungles of Borneo by a missionary. It is a naturally occurring antibiotic made by the soil bacterium Actinobacteria species Amycolatopsis orientalis (formerly designated Nocardia orientalis).

Infection	Infection is the invasion of a host organism's bodily tissues by disease-causing organisms, their multiplication, and the reaction of host tissues to these organisms and the toxins they produce. Infections are caused by microorganisms such as viruses, prions, bacteria, and viroids, and larger organisms like macroparasites and fungi. Hosts can fight infections using their immune system.
Antimicrobial	An antimicrobial is an agent that kills microorganisms or inhibits their growth. Antimicrobial medicines can be grouped according to the microorganisms they act primarily against. For example, antibacterials are used against bacteria and antifungals are used against fungi.
Cefuroxime	Cefuroxime is a parenteral second generation cephalosporin antibiotic. It was discovered by Glaxo now GlaxoSmithKline and introduced in 1978 as Zinacef. It was approved by FDA on 19 Oct 1983. In US it is available as Zinacef by Covis Pharmaceuticals as the company acquired the US rights of the product from GSK. In India it is available as Supacef by GSK. Cefuroxime axetil is an acetoxyetyl ester prodrug of cefuroxime which is effective orally.
Chancroid	Chancroid is a bacterial sexually transmitted infection characterized by painful sores on the genitalia. Chancroid is known to spread from one individual to another solely through sexual contact.
Dicloxacillin	Dicloxacillin is a narrow-spectrum beta-lactam antibiotic of the penicillin class. It is used to treat infections caused by susceptible Gram-positive bacteria. It is active against beta-lactamase-producing organisms such as Staphylococcus aureus, which would otherwise be resistant to most penicillins.
Erythromycin	Erythromycin is a macrolide antibiotic that has an antimicrobial spectrum similar to or slightly wider than that of penicillin, and is often prescribed for people who have an allergy to penicillins. For respiratory tract infections, it has better coverage of atypical organisms, including Mycoplasma and legionellosis. It was first marketed by Eli Lilly and Company, and it is today commonly known as EES (erythromycin ethylsuccinate, an ester prodrug that is commonly administered).
Gonorrhea	Gonorrhea is a common human sexually transmitted infection caused by the bacterium Neisseria gonorrhoeae. The usual symptoms in men are burning with urination and penile discharge. Women, on the other hand, are asymptomatic half the time or have vaginal discharge and pelvic pain.
Penicillin	Penicillin is a group of antibiotics derived from Penicillium fungi. They include penicillin G, procaine penicillin, benzathine penicillin, and penicillin V. Penicillin antibiotics are historically significant because they are the first drugs that were effective against many previously serious diseases, such as syphilis, and infections caused by staphylococci and streptococci. Penicillins are still widely used today, though many types of bacteria are now resistant.

14. UNIT-14 Antiinfectives,

Rocky Mountain spotted fever	Rocky Mountain spotted fever is the most lethal and most frequently reported rickettsial illness in the United States. It has been diagnosed throughout the Americas. Some synonyms for Rocky Mountain spotted fever in other countries include "tick typhus," "Tobia fever" (Colombia), "São Paulo fever" or "febre maculosa" (Brazil), and "fiebre manchada" (Mexico).
Peptic ulcer disease	A peptic ulcer, also known as peptic ulcer disease is the most common ulcer of an area of the gastrointestinal tract that is usually acidic and thus extremely painful. It is defined as mucosal erosions equal to or greater than 0.5 cm. As many as 70-90% of such ulcers are associated with Helicobacter pylori, a helical-shaped bacterium that lives in the acidic environment of the stomach; however, only 40% of those cases go to a doctor.
Central nervous system	The central nervous system is the part of the nervous system that integrates the information that it receives from, and coordinates the activity of, all parts of the bodies of bilaterian animals-that is, all multicellular animals except radially symmetric animals such as sponges and jellyfish. It contains the majority of the nervous system and consists of the brain and the spinal cord. Some classifications also include the retina and the cranial nerves in the Central nervous system. Together with the peripheral nervous system, it has a fundamental role in the control of behavior.
Nafcillin	Nafcillin sodium is a narrow-spectrum beta-lactam antibiotic of the penicillin class. As a beta-lactamase-resistant penicillin, it is used to treat infections caused by Gram-positive bacteria, in particular, species of staphylococci that are resistant to other penicillins. Nafcillin is considered therapeutically equivalent to oxacillin, although its safety profile is somewhat different.
Oxacillin	Oxacillin sodium is a narrow spectrum beta-lactam antibiotic of the penicillin class. It was developed by Beecham.
Penicillin G	Benzylpenicillin, commonly known as penicillin G, is the gold standard type of penicillin. 'G' in the name 'Penicillin G' refers to 'Gold Standard'. Penicillin G is typically given by a parenteral route of administration (not orally) because it is unstable in the hydrochloric acid of the stomach.
Piperacillin	Piperacillin is an extended-spectrum beta-lactam antibiotic of the ureidopenicillin class. It is normally used together with a beta-lactamase inhibitor, notably in the combination piperacillin/tazobactam.
Ticarcillin	Ticarcillin is a carboxypenicillin. It is almost invariably sold and used in combination with clavulanate as Timentin. Because it is a penicillin, it also falls within the larger class of beta-lactam antibiotics.
Mechanism of action	In pharmacology, the term mechanism of action refers to the specific biochemical interaction through which a drug substance produces its pharmacological effect.

	A mechanism of action usually includes mention of the specific molecular targets to which the drug binds, such as an enzyme or receptor.
	For example, the mechanism of action of aspirin involves irreversible inhibition of the enzyme cyclooxygenase, therefore suppressing the production of prostaglandins and thromboxanes, thereby reducing pain and inflammation.
Cefdinir	Cefdinir is a third generation oral cephalosporin antibiotic. It was discovered by Fujisawa Pharmaceutical Co., Ltd. 'Fujisawa' (now Astellas) and introduced in 1991 under the brand name Cefzon.
Ceftibuten	Ceftibuten is a third-generation cephalosporin antibiotic. It is an orally-administered agent, with 2 dosage forms, capsule or oral suspension. It is marketed by Pernix Therapeutics under the trade name Cedax.
Allergy	An allergy is a hypersensitivity disorder of the immune system. Allergic reactions occur when a person's immune system reacts to normally harmless substances in the environment. A substance that causes a reaction is called an allergen.
Cephalexin	Cefalexin or cephalexin is an antibiotic useful for the treatment of a number of bacterial infections. It is taken by mouth and is active against Gram-positive bacteria and some Gram-negative bacteria. It is in the class of first-generation cephalosporins and has similar activity to other agents within this group, including the intravenous agent cefazolin.
Doxycycline	Doxycycline is a member of the tetracycline antibiotics group, and is commonly used to treat a variety of infections. Doxycycline is a semisynthetic tetracycline invented and clinically developed in the early 1960s by Pfizer Inc. and marketed under the brand name Vibramycin.
Pharmacokinetics	Pharmacokinetics, is a branch of pharmacology dedicated to the determination of the fate of substances administered externally to a living organism. The substances of interest include pharmaceutical agents, hormones, nutrients, and toxins.
	Pharmacokinetics includes the study of the mechanisms of absorption and distribution of an administered drug, the chemical changes of the substance in the body (e.g. by metabolic enzymes such as CYP or UGT enzymes), and the effects and routes of excretion of the metabolites of the drug.
Tetracycline	Tetracycline ( ) is a broad-spectrum polyketide antibiotic produced by the Streptomyces genus of Actinobacteria, indicated for use against many bacterial infections. It is a protein synthesis inhibitor. It is commonly used to treat acne today, and, more recently, rosacea, and is historically important in reducing the number of deaths from cholera.
Fidaxomicin	Fidaxomicin is the first in a new class of narrow spectrum macrocyclic antibiotic drugs.

	It is a fermentation product obtained from the actinomycete Dactylosporangium aurantiacum subspecies hamdenesis. Fidaxomicin is non-systemic, meaning it is minimally absorbed into the bloodstream, it is bactericidal, and it has demonstrated selective eradication of pathogenic Clostridium difficile with minimal disruption to the multiple species of bacteria that make up the normal, healthy intestinal flora.
Macrolide	The macrolides are a group of drugs (typically antibiotics) whose activity stems from the presence of a macrolide ring, a large macrocyclic lactone ring to which one or more deoxy sugars, usually cladinose and desosamine, may be attached. The lactone rings are usually 14-, 15-, or 16-membered. Macrolides belong to the polyketide class of natural products.
Telithromycin	Telithromycin is the first ketolide antibiotic to enter clinical use and is sold under the brand name of Ketek. It is used to treat community acquired pneumonia of mild to moderate severity. After significant controversy regarding safety and research fraud, the US Food and Drug Administration sharply curtailed the approved uses of the drug in 2007.
Norfloxacin	Norfloxacin is a synthetic chemotherapeutic antibacterial agent occasionally used to treat common as well as complicated urinary tract infections. It is sold under various brand names with the most common being Noroxin. In form of ophthalmic solutions it is known as Chibroxin.
Kanamycin	Kanamycin is an aminoglycoside bacteriocidal antibiotic, available in oral, intravenous, and intramuscular forms, and used to treat a wide variety of infections. Kanamycin is isolated from the bacterium Streptomyces kanamyceticus and its most commonly used form is kanamycin sulfate.
Sulfamethoxazole	Sulfamethoxazole is a sulfonamide bacteriostatic antibiotic. It is most often used as part of a synergistic combination with trimethoprim in a 5:1 ratio in co-trimoxazole , also known under trade names such as Bactrim, Septrin, or Septra; in Eastern Europe it is marketed as Biseptol. Its primary activity is against susceptible forms of Streptococcus, Staphylococcus aureus (including MRSA), Escherichia coli, Haemophilus influenzae, and oral anaerobes.
Sulfisoxazole	Sulfafurazole (INN, also known as sulfisoxazole) is a sulfonamide antibacterial with an oxazole substituent. It has antibiotic activity against a wide range of Gram-negative and Gram-positive organisms. It is sometimes given in combination with erythromycin or phenazopyridine.
Ethambutol	Ethambutol is a bacteriostatic antimycobacterial drug prescribed to treat tuberculosis. It is usually given in combination with other tuberculosis drugs, such as isoniazid, rifampicin and pyrazinamide. It is sold under the trade names Myambutol and Servambutol.
Risk factor	In epidemiology, a risk factor is a variable associated with an increased risk of disease or infection.

	Sometimes, determinant is also used, being a variable associated with either increased or decreased risk.
Tuberculosis treatment	Tuberculosis treatment refers to the medical treatment of the infectious disease tuberculosis . The standard 'short' course treatment for TB is isoniazid (along with pyridoxal phosphate to obviate peripheral neuropathy caused by isoniazid), rifampicin (also known as rifampin in the United States), pyrazinamide, and ethambutol for two months, then isoniazid and rifampicin alone for a further four months. The patient is considered to be free of living bacteria after six months (although there is still a relapse rate of up to 7%).
Pyrazinamide	Pyrazinamide is a drug used to treat tuberculosis. The drug is largely bacteriostatic, but can be bacteriocidal on actively replicating tuberculosis bacteria.
Rifabutin	Rifabutin is a bactericidal antibiotic drug primarily used in the treatment of tuberculosis. The drug is a semi-synthetic derivative of rifamycin S. Its effect is based on blocking the DNA-dependent RNA-polymerase of the bacteria. It is effective against Gram-positive and some Gram-negative bacteria, but also against the highly resistant Mycobacteria, e.g. Mycobacterium tuberculosis, M. leprae, and M. avium intracellulare.
Rifampicin	Rifampicin (INN) or rifampin is a bactericidal antibiotic drug of the rifamycin group. It is a semisynthetic compound derived from Amycolatopsis rifamycinica (formerly known as Amycolatopsis mediterranei and Streptomyces mediterranei). Rifampicin may be abbreviated R, RMP, RA, RF, or RIF (US).
Rifapentine	Rifapentine (INN, marketed under the brand name Priftin by Sanofi-Aventis) is an antibiotic drug used in the treatment of tuberculosis. Rifapentine was first synthesized in 1965 by the same company that produced rifampin. The drug was approved by the Food and Drug Administration (FDA) in June 1998. It is synthesized in one step from rifampicine.
Capreomycin	Capreomycin is a peptide antibiotic, commonly grouped with the aminoglycosides, which is given in combination with other antibiotics for MDR-tuberculosis. Adverse effects include nephrotoxicity and 8th cranial auditory vestibular nerve nerve toxicity. The drug should not be given with streptomycin or other drugs that may damage the auditory vestibular nerve.
Cycloserine	Cycloserine is an antibiotic effective against Mycobacterium tuberculosis. For the treatment of tuberculosis, it is classified as a second line drug, i.e. its use is only considered if one or more first line drugs cannot be used.

14. UNIT-14 Antiinfectives,

Ethionamide	Ethionamide (2-ethylthioisonicotinamide, Trecator SC) is an antibiotic used in the treatment of tuberculosis. It was discovered in 1956. Ethionamide works to induce expression of EthA, a NAD derivative which is toxic to the bacteria.
Anidulafungin	Anidulafungin is a semisynthetic echinocandin used as an antifungal drug. Anidulafungin was originally manufactured and submitted for FDA approval by Vicuron Pharmaceuticals. Pfizer acquired the drug upon its acquisition of Vicuron in the fall of 2005. Pfizer gained approval by the Food and Drug Administration (FDA) on February 21, 2006; it was previously known as LY303366. There is preliminary evidence it has a similar safety profile to caspofungin.
Azole	An azole is a class of five-membered nitrogen heterocyclic ring compounds containing at least one other non-carbon atom of either nitrogen, sulfur, or oxygen. The parent compounds are aromatic and have two double bonds; there are successively reduced analogs (azolines and azolidines) with fewer. One, and only one, lone pair of electrons from each heteroatom in the ring is part of the aromatic bonding in an azole.
Griseofulvin	Griseofulvin (marketed under the proprietary name Grifulvin V by Orthoneutrogena Labs, according to FDA orange book) is an antifungal drug that is administered orally. It is used both in animals and in humans, to treat fungal infections of the skin (commonly known as ringworm) and nails. It is produced by culture of some strains of the mold Penicillium griseofulvum, from which it was isolated in 1939.
Fungal	A fungus is a member of a large group of eukaryotic organisms that includes microorganisms such as yeasts and molds, as well as the more familiar mushrooms. These organisms are classified as a kingdom, Fungi, which is separate from plants, animals, and bacteria. One major difference is that fungal cells have cell walls that contain chitin, unlike the cell walls of plants, which contain cellulose.
Topical	In medicine, a topical medication is applied to body surfaces such as the skin or mucous membranes such as the vagina, anus, throat, eyes and ears. Many topical medications are epicutaneous, meaning that they are applied directly to the skin. Topical medications may also be inhalational, such as asthma medications, or applied to the surface of tissues other than the skin, such as eye drops applied to the conjunctiva, or ear drops placed in the ear, or medications applied to the surface of a tooth.
Antiretroviral	The management of HIV/AIDS normally includes the use of multiple antiretroviral drugs in an attempt to control HIV infection. There are several classes of antiretroviral agents that act on different stages of the HIV life-cycle. The use of multiple drugs that act on different viral targets is known as highly active antiretroviral therapy (HAART).

Atazanavir	Atazanavir, marketed under the trade name Reyataz by Bristol Myers, (formerly known as BMS-232632) is an antiretroviral drug of the protease inhibitor (PI) class. Like other antiretrovirals, it is used to treat infection of human immunodeficiency virus (HIV).
	Atazanavir is distinguished from other PIs in that it can be given once-daily (rather than requiring multiple doses per day) and has lesser effects on the patient's lipid profile (the amounts of cholesterol and other fatty substances in the blood).
Darunavir	Darunavir is a drug used to treat HIV infection. It is in the protease inhibitor class. Prezista is an OARAC recommended treatment option for treatment-naïve and treatment-experienced adults and adolescents.
Delavirdine	Delavirdine (brand name Rescriptor) is a non-nucleoside reverse transcriptase inhibitor (NNRTI) marketed by ViiV Healthcare. It is used as part of highly active antiretroviral therapy (HAART) for the treatment of human immunodeficiency virus (HIV) type 1. It is presented as the mesylate. The recommended dosage is 400 mg, three times a day.
Enfuvirtide	Enfuvirtide (INN) is an HIV fusion inhibitor, the first of a novel class of antiretroviral drugs used in combination therapy for the treatment of HIV-1 infection. It is marketed under the trade name Fuzeon.
	Enfuvirtide therapy costs an estimated US$25,000 per year in the United States.
Indinavir	Indinavir (IDV; trade name Crixivan, manufactured by Merck) is a protease inhibitor used as a component of highly active antiretroviral therapy (HAART) to treat HIV infection and AIDS.
	The Food and Drug Administration (FDA) approved indinavir March 13, 1996, making it the eighth approved antiretroviral. Indinavir was much more powerful than any prior antiretroviral drug; using it with dual NRTIs set the standard for treatment of HIV/AIDS and raised the bar on design and introduction of subsequent antiretroviral drugs. Protease inhibitors changed the very nature of the AIDS epidemic from one of a terminal illness to a somewhat manageable one.
Lamivudine	Lamivudine (2',3'-dideoxy-3'-thiacytidine, commonly called 3TC) is a potent nucleoside analog reverse transcriptase inhibitor (nRTI).
	It is marketed by GlaxoSmithKline with the brand names Zeffix, Heptovir, Epivir, and Epivir-HBV.
	Lamivudine has been used for treatment of chronic hepatitis B at a lower dose than for treatment of HIV. It improves the seroconversion of e-antigen positive hepatitis B and also improves histology staging of the liver. Long term use of lamivudine unfortunately leads to emergence of a resistant hepatitis B virus (YMDD) mutant.

14. UNIT-14 Antiinfectives,

Nevirapine	Nevirapine also marketed under the trade name Viramune (Boehringer Ingelheim), is a non-nucleoside reverse transcriptase inhibitor (NNRTI) used to treat HIV-1 infection and AIDS. As with other antiretroviral drugs, HIV rapidly develops resistance if nevirapine is used alone, so recommended therapy consists of combinations of three or more antiretrovirals. Nevirapine was discovered by Hargrave et al. at Boehringer Ingelheim Pharmaceuticals, Inc., one of the Boehringer Ingelheim group of companies. It is covered by U.S. Patent 5,366,972 and corresponding foreign patents.
Protease inhibitor	In biology and biochemistry, protease inhibitors are molecules that inhibit the function of proteases. Many naturally occurring protease inhibitors are proteins. In medicine, protease inhibitor is often used interchangeably with alpha 1-antitrypsin .
Raltegravir	Raltegravir is an antiretroviral drug produced by Merck & Co., used to treat HIV infection. It received approval by the U.S. Food and Drug Administration (FDA) on 12 October 2007, the first of a new class of HIV drugs, the integrase inhibitors, to receive such approval. In December 2011, it received FDA approval for pediatric use in patients ages 2-18, taken in pill form orally twice a day by prescription with two other antiretroviral medications to form the cocktail (most anti-HIV drugs regimens for adults and children use these cocktails).
Stavudine	Stavudine is a nucleoside analog reverse transcriptase inhibitor (NARTI) active against HIV.
Zidovudine	Zidovudine or azidothymidine (AZT) (also called ZDV) is a nucleoside analog reverse-transcriptase inhibitor (NRTI), a type of antiretroviral drug used for the treatment of HIVAIDS. It is an analog of thymidine. AZT was the first approved treatment for HIV, sold under the names Retrovir and Retrovis. AZT use was a major breakthrough in AIDS therapy in the 1990s that significantly altered the course of the illness and helped destroy the notion that HIV/AIDS was a death sentence.
Oseltamivir	Oseltamivir INN, marketed under the trade name Tamiflu, is an antiviral drug, which may slow the spread of influenza (flu) virus between cells in the body by stopping the virus from chemically cutting ties with its host cell. The drug is taken orally in capsules or as a suspension. It is used to treat influenza A virus and influenza B virus.
Rimantadine	Rimantadine is an orally administered antiviral drug used to treat, and in rare cases prevent, influenzavirus A infection. When taken within one to two days of developing symptoms, rimantadine can shorten the duration and moderate the severity of influenza.

14. UNIT-14 Antiinfectives,

Tinidazole	Tinidazole is an anti-parasitic drug used against protozoan infections. It is widely known throughout Europe and the developing world as a treatment for a variety of amoebic and parasitic infections. It was developed in 1972.
Zanamivir	Zanamivir INN is a neuraminidase inhibitor used in the treatment and prophylaxis of influenza caused by influenza A virus and influenza B virus. Zanamivir was the first neuraminidase inhibitor commercially developed. It is currently marketed by GlaxoSmithKline under the trade name Relenza as a powder for oral inhalation.
Herpes simplex	Herpes simplex is a viral disease from the herpesviridae family caused by both Herpes simplex virus type 1 (HSV-1) and type 2 (HSV-2). Infection with the herpes virus is categorized into one of several distinct disorders based on the site of infection. Oral herpes, the visible symptoms of which are colloquially called 'cold sores' or 'fever blisters', is an infection of the face or mouth.
Malaria	Malaria is a mosquito-borne infectious disease of humans and other animals caused by parasitic protozoans of the genus Plasmodium. Commonly, the disease is transmitted by a bite from an infected female Anopheles mosquito, which introduces the organisms from its saliva into a person's circulatory system. In the blood, the parasites travel to the liver to mature and reproduce.
Chloroquine	Chloroquine is a 4-aminoquinoline drug used in the treatment or prevention of malaria.

CHAPTER QUIZ: KEY TERMS, PEOPLE, PLACES, CONCEPTS

1. The _____s are a group of drugs (typically antibiotics) whose activity stems from the presence of a _____ ring, a large macrocyclic lactone ring to which one or more deoxy sugars, usually cladinose and desosamine, may be attached. The lactone rings are usually 14-, 15-, or 16-membered. _____s belong to the polyketide class of natural products.

   a. Bryostatin
   b. Kendomycin
   c. Lucimycin
   d. Macrolide

2. . A peptic ulcer, also known as _____ is the most common ulcer of an area of the gastrointestinal tract that is usually acidic and thus extremely painful. It is defined as mucosal erosions equal to or greater than 0.5 cm. As many as 70-90% of such ulcers are associated with Helicobacter pylori, a helical-shaped bacterium that lives in the acidic environment of the stomach; however, only 40% of those cases go to a doctor.

   a. Peptic ulcer

b. Dyspepsia

c. Peptic ulcer disease

d. Gastric ulcer

3. _____ is a third-generation cephalosporin antibiotic. It is an orally-administered agent, with 2 dosage forms, capsule or oral suspension. It is marketed by Pernix Therapeutics under the trade name Cedax.

   a. Ceftibuten
   b. Suprax
   c. Cedax
   d. Cefditoren

4. _____, marketed under the trade name Reyataz by Bristol Myers, (formerly known as BMS-232632) is an antiretroviral drug of the protease inhibitor (PI) class. Like other antiretrovirals, it is used to treat infection of human immunodeficiency virus (HIV).

   _____ is distinguished from other PIs in that it can be given once-daily (rather than requiring multiple doses per day) and has lesser effects on the patient's lipid profile (the amounts of cholesterol and other fatty substances in the blood).

   a. isomer
   b. liposome
   c. Atazanavir
   d. Liniment

5. Sulfafurazole (INN, also known as _____) is a sulfonamide antibacterial with an oxazole substituent. It has antibiotic activity against a wide range of Gram-negative and Gram-positive organisms. It is sometimes given in combination with erythromycin or phenazopyridine.

   a. Bactocill
   b. Homeopathic
   c. Sulfisoxazole
   d. Penicillin V

---

1. d
2. c
3. a
4. c
5. c

You can take the complete Online Interactive Chapter Practice Test

for 14. UNIT-14 Antiinfectives,
on all key terms, persons, places, and concepts.

No Additional Costs

http://www.Cram101.com

Register, send an email request to Travis.Reese@Cram101.com to get your user Id and password.

Include your customer order number, and ISBN number from your studyguide Retailer.

15. UNIT-1S Health Promotion

CHAPTER OUTLINE: KEY TERMS, PEOPLE, PLACES, CONCEPTS

Herpes zoster

Pharmacokinetics

Diphtheria

Immunization

Granulocyte

Mast cell

Immunoglobulin

Cell-mediated

Thyroid hormone

Hepatitis B vaccine

Vaccine

Tetanus vaccine

Rubella vaccine

Varicella vaccine

Influenza vaccine

Hepatitis A vaccine

Meningococcal vaccine

Human papilloma viru

Typhoid vaccine

Sympathomimetic

Stimulant

	Body mass index
	Metabolic syndrome
	Nicotine
	Varenicline
	Nicotine nasal spray
	Drug interaction
	Phosphorus
	Pyridoxine
	Vitamin C
	Cobalt
	Iodine
	Iron
	Magnesium
	Manganese
	Potassium
	Sulfur
	Vitamin E
	Retinol
	Ergocalciferol
	Toxicity

Herpes zoster	Herpes zoster, commonly known as shingles and also known as zona, is a viral disease characterized by a painful skin rash with blisters in a limited area on one side of the body (left or right), often in a stripe. The initial infection with varicella zoster virus (VZV) causes the acute, short-lived illness chickenpox which generally occurs in children and young adults. Once an episode of chickenpox has resolved, the virus is not eliminated from the body and can go on to cause herpes zoster often many years after the initial infection.
Pharmacokinetics	Pharmacokinetics, is a branch of pharmacology dedicated to the determination of the fate of substances administered externally to a living organism. The substances of interest include pharmaceutical agents, hormones, nutrients, and toxins.
	Pharmacokinetics includes the study of the mechanisms of absorption and distribution of an administered drug, the chemical changes of the substance in the body (e.g. by metabolic enzymes such as CYP or UGT enzymes), and the effects and routes of excretion of the metabolites of the drug.
Diphtheria	Diphtheria (Greek διφθ?ρα (diphthera) 'pair of leather scrolls') is an upper respiratory tract illness caused by Corynebacterium diphtheriae, a facultative anaerobic, Gram-positive bacterium. It is characterized by sore throat, low fever, and an adherent membrane (a pseudomembrane) on the tonsils, pharynx, and/or nasal cavity. A milder form of diphtheria can be restricted to the skin.
Immunization	Immunization, is the process by which an individual's immune system becomes fortified against an agent (known as the immunogen).
	When this system is exposed to molecules that are foreign to the body, called non-self, it will orchestrate an immune response, and it will also develop the ability to quickly respond to a subsequent encounter because of immunological memory. This is a function of the adaptive immune system.
Granulocyte	Granulocytes are a category of white blood cells characterized by the presence of granules in their cytoplasm. They are also called polymorphonuclear leukocytes (PMN, PML, or PMNL) because of the varying shapes of the nucleus, which is usually lobed into three segments. This distinguishes them from the mononuclear agranulocytes.
Mast cell	A mast cell is derived from the myeloid stem cell and a part of the immune system that contains many granules rich in histamine and heparin. Although best known for their role in allergy and anaphylaxis, mast cells play an important protective role as well, being intimately involved in wound healing and defense against pathogens.
	The mast cell is very similar in both appearance and function to the basophil, another type of white blood cell.

15. UNIT-1S Health Promotion

Immunoglobulin	An antibody, also known as an immunoglobulin is a large Y-shape protein produced by plasma cells that is used by the immune system to identify and neutralize foreign objects such as bacteria and viruses. The antibody recognizes a unique part of the foreign target, called an antigen. Each tip of the 'Y' of an antibody contains a paratope (a structure analogous to a lock) that is specific for one particular epitope (similarly analogous to a key) on an antigen, allowing these two structures to bind together with precision.
Cell-mediated	Cell-mediated immunity is an immune response that does not involve antibodies, but rather involves the activation of phagocytes, antigen-specific cytotoxic T-lymphocytes, and the release of various cytokines in response to an antigen. Historically, the immune system was separated into two branches: humoral immunity, for which the protective function of immunization could be found in the humor (cell-free bodily fluid or serum) and cellular immunity, for which the protective function of immunization was associated with cells. CD4 cells or helper T cells provide protection against different pathogens.
Thyroid hormone	The thyroid hormones, triiodothyronine and its prohormone, thyroxine (T_4), are tyrosine-based hormones produced by the thyroid gland that are primarily responsible for regulation of metabolism. Iodine is necessary for the production of T_3 and T_4. A deficiency of iodine leads to decreased production of T_3 and T_4, enlarges the thyroid tissue and will cause the disease known as simple goitre.
Hepatitis B vaccine	Hepatitis B vaccine is a vaccine developed for the prevention of hepatitis B virus infection. The vaccine contains one of the viral envelope proteins, hepatitis B surface antigen (HBsAg). It is produced by yeast cells, into which the genetic code for HBsAg has been inserted.
Vaccine	A vaccine is a biological preparation that improves immunity to a particular disease. A vaccine typically contains an agent that resembles a disease-causing microorganism, and is often made from weakened or killed forms of the microbe, its toxins or one of its surface proteins. The agent stimulates the body's immune system to recognize the agent as foreign, destroy it, and 'remember' it, so that the immune system can more easily recognize and destroy any of these microorganisms that it later encounters.
Tetanus vaccine	Tetanus vaccine is a vaccine composed of inactivated tetanus toxin with formaldehyde. This vaccine is imumunogenic not pathogenic and is used to prevent an individual from contracting tetanus. Tetanus, also known as lockjaw, is a disease caused by the bacteria Clostridium tetani which enters the body through open wounds and releases a poison called tetanospasmin.
Rubella vaccine	Rubella vaccine is a vaccine used against rubella. One form is called 'Meruvax'.
Varicella vaccine	The varicella vaccine is a live (attenuated) virus that protects against the viral disease commonly known as chickenpox caused by Varicella Zoster Virus (VZV). Varicella vaccine is marketed as Varivax in the U.S. by Merck.

Influenza vaccine	The influenza vaccination is an annual vaccination using a vaccine specific for a given year to protect against the highly variable influenza virus. Each seasonal influenza vaccine contains antigens representing three or four influenza virus strains: one influenza type A subtype H1N1 virus strain, one influenza type A subtype H3N2 virus strain, and either one or two influenza type B virus strains. Influenza vaccines may be administered as an injection, also known as a flu shot, or as a nasal spray.
Hepatitis A vaccine	Hepatitis A vaccine is a vaccine against the hepatitis A virus. The first successful vaccine against it was invented by Maurice Hilleman at Merck. The vaccine protects against the virus in more than 95% of cases and provides protection from the virus for at least ten years.
Meningococcal vaccine	Meningococcal vaccine is a vaccine used against Neisseria meningitidis, a bacterium that causes meningitis, meningococcemia, septicemia, and rarely carditis, septic arthritis, or pneumonia.
Human papilloma viru	The human papilloma virus vaccine prevents infection with certain species of human papillomavirus associated with the development of cervical cancer, genital warts, and some less common cancers. Two Human papillomavirus vaccine vaccines are currently on the market: Gardasil and Cervarix.

Both vaccines protect against the two Human papillomavirus vaccine types (Human papillomavirus vaccine-16 and Human papillomavirus vaccine-18) that cause 70% of cervical cancers, 80% of anal cancers, 60% of vaginal cancers, and 40% of vulvar cancers. |
| Typhoid vaccine | Typhoid vaccine is a vaccine used against typhoid.

Types include:•Ty21a, which is a live vaccine•Vi capsular polysaccharide vaccine, which is a subunit vaccine. |
| Sympathomimetic | Sympathomimetic drugs mimic the effects of transmitter substances of the sympathetic nervous system such as catecholamines, epinephrine (adrenaline), norepinephrine (noradrenaline), dopamine, etc. Such drugs are used to treat cardiac arrest and low blood pressure, or even delay premature labor, among other things.

These drugs act at the postganglionic sympathetic terminal, either directly activating postsynaptic receptors, blocking breakdown and reuptake, or stimulating production and release of catecholamines. |
| Stimulant | Stimulants (also referred to as psychostimulants) are psychoactive drugs which induce temporary improvements in either mental or physical functions or both. Examples of these kinds of effects may include enhanced alertness, wakefulness, and locomotion, among others. Due to their effects typically having an 'up' quality to them, stimulants are also occasionally referred to as 'uppers'. |

15. UNIT-1S Health Promotion

Body mass index	The body mass index, or Quetelet index, is a measure of relative weight based on an individual's mass and height.
	Devised between 1830 and 1850 by the Belgian polymath Adolphe Quetelet during the course of developing 'social physics', it is defined as the individual's body mass divided by the square of their height - with the value universally being given in units of kg/m^2.
	Body mass index can also be determined using a table or from a chart which displays Body mass index as a function of mass and height using contour lines, or colors for different Body mass index categories, and may use two different units of measurement.
Metabolic syndrome	Metabolic syndrome is a disorder of energy utilization and storage, diagnosed by a co-occurrence of three out of five of the following medical conditions: abdominal obesity, elevated blood pressure, elevated fasting plasma glucose, high serum triglycerides, and low high-density cholesterol (HDL) levels. Metabolic syndrome increases the risk of developing cardiovascular disease, particularly heart failure, and diabetes. Some studies have shown the prevalence in the USA to be an estimated 34% of the adult population, and the prevalence increases with age.
Nicotine	Nicotine is an alkaloid found in the nightshade family of plants (Solanaceae) that constitutes approximately 0.6-3.0% of the dry weight of tobacco, with biosynthesis taking place in the roots and accumulation occurring in the leaves. It functions as an antiherbivore chemical with particular specificity to insects; therefore nicotine was widely used as an insecticide in the past, and currently nicotine analogs such as imidacloprid continue to be widely used.
	In low concentrations (an average cigarette yields about 1 mg of absorbed nicotine), the substance acts as a stimulant in mammals and is the main factor responsible for the dependence-forming properties of tobacco smoking.
Varenicline	Varenicline (trade name Chantix in the USA and Champix in Canada, Europe and other countries, marketed by Pfizer, usually in the form of varenicline tartrate), is a prescription medication used to treat smoking addiction. Varenicline is a nicotinic receptor partial agonist - it stimulates nicotine receptors more weakly than nicotine itself does. In this respect it is similar to cytisine and different from the nicotinic antagonist, bupropion, and nicotine replacement therapies (NRTs) like nicotine patches and nicotine gum.
Nicotine nasal spray	A nicotine nasal spray is a nasal spray that contains a small dose of nicotine, which enters the blood by being absorbed through the lining of the nose. This helps stop nicotine cravings and relieves symptoms that occur when a person is trying to quit smoking. A prescription is needed for nicotine nasal spray in many countries.
Drug interaction	A drug interaction is a situation in which a substance affects the activity of a drug, i.e. the effects are increased or decreased, or they produce a new effect that neither produces on its own.

	Typically, interaction between drugs come to mind (drug-drug interaction). However, interactions may also exist between drugs & foods (drug-food interactions), as well as drugs & herbs (drug-herb interactions).People taking antidepressant drugs such as Monoamine oxidase inhibitors should not take food containing tyramine.Hypertensive crisis may occur(An example of drug-food interactions).
Phosphorus	Phosphorus is a chemical element with symbol P and atomic number 15. A multivalent nonmetal of the nitrogen group, phosphorus as a mineral is almost always present in its maximally oxidised state, as inorganic phosphate rocks. Elemental phosphorus exists in two major forms-white phosphorus and red phosphorus-but due to its high reactivity, phosphorus is never found as a free element on Earth.
	The first form of elemental phosphorus to be produced (white phosphorus, in 1669) emits a faint glow upon exposure to oxygen - hence its name given from Greek mythology, meaning 'light-bearer', referring to the 'Morning Star', the planet Venus.
Pyridoxine	Pyridoxine is one of the compounds that can be called vitamin B_6, along with pyridoxal and pyridoxamine. It differs from pyridoxamine by the substituent at the '4' position. Its hydrochloride salt pyridoxine hydrochloride is often used.
Vitamin C	Vitamin C or -ascorbic acid, or simply ascorbate, is an essential nutrient for humans and certain other animal species. Vitamin C refers to a number of vitamers that have vitamin C activity in animals, including ascorbic acid and its salts, and some oxidized forms of the molecule like dehydroascorbic acid. Ascorbate and ascorbic acid are both naturally present in the body when either of these is introduced into cells, since the forms interconvert according to pH.
	Vitamin C is a cofactor in at least eight enzymatic reactions, including several collagen synthesis reactions that, when dysfunctional, cause the most severe symptoms of scurvy.
Cobalt	Cobalt is a chemical element with symbol Co and atomic number 27. It is found naturally only in chemically combined form. The free element, produced by reductive smelting, is a hard, lustrous, silver-gray metal.
	Cobalt-based blue pigments (cobalt blue) have been used since ancient times for jewelry and paints, and to impart a distinctive blue tint to glass, but the color was later thought by alchemists to be due to the known metal bismuth.
Iodine	Iodine is a chemical element with symbol I and atomic number 53. The name is from Greek ioeides, meaning violet or purple, due to the color of elemental iodine vapor.
	Iodine and its compounds are primarily used in nutrition, and industrially in the production of acetic acid and certain polymers.

15. UNIT-1S Health Promotion

Iron	Iron is a chemical element with the symbol Fe and atomic number 26. It is a metal in the first transition series. It is the most common element (by mass) forming the planet Earth as a whole, forming much of Earth's outer and inner core. It is the fourth most common element in the Earth's crust.
Magnesium	Magnesium is a chemical element with the symbol Mg and atomic number 12. Its common oxidation number is +2. It is an alkaline earth metal and the eighth most abundant element in the Earth's crust and ninth in the known universe as a whole. Magnesium is the fourth most common element in the Earth as a whole (behind iron, oxygen and silicon), making up 13% of the planet's mass and a large fraction of the planet's mantle. The relative abundance of magnesium is related to the fact that it easily builds up in supernova stars from a sequential addition of three helium nuclei to carbon (which in turn is made from three helium nuclei).
Manganese	Manganese is a chemical element, designated by the symbol Mn. It has the atomic number 25. It is found as a free element in nature (often in combination with iron), and in many minerals. Manganese is a metal with important industrial metal alloy uses, particularly in stainless steels.
Potassium	Potassium is a chemical element with symbol K and atomic number 19. Elemental potassium is a soft silvery-white alkali metal that oxidizes rapidly in air and is very reactive with water, generating sufficient heat to ignite the hydrogen emitted in the reaction and burning with a lilac flame. Because potassium and sodium are chemically very similar, their salts were not at first differentiated. The existence of multiple elements in their salts was suspected from 1702, and this was proven in 1807 when potassium and sodium were individually isolated from different salts by electrolysis.
Sulfur	Sulfur is a chemical element with symbol S and atomic number 16. It is an abundant, multivalent non-metal. Under normal conditions, sulfur atoms form cyclic octatomic molecules with chemical formula S_8. Elemental sulfur is a bright yellow crystalline solid when at room temperature.
Vitamin E	Vitamin E refers to a group of ten lipid-soluble compounds that include both tocopherols and tocotrienols. Of the many different forms of vitamin E, ?-tocopherol is the most common in the North American diet. ?-Tocopherol can be found in corn oil, soybean oil, margarine, and dressings.
Retinol	Retinol is one of the animal forms of vitamin A. It is a diterpenoid and an alcohol. It is convertible to other forms of vitamin A, and the retinyl ester derivative of the alcohol serves as the storage form of the vitamin in animals. When converted to the retinal (retinaldehyde) form, vitamin A is essential for vision, and when converted to retinoic acid is essential for skin health, teeth remineralization and bone growth.
Ergocalciferol	Ergocalciferol is the chemical name of vitamin D_2, a form of vitamin D.

Ergocalciferol is a secosteroid formed by a photochemical bond breaking of a steroid, specifically, by the action of ultraviolet light on ergosterol. Viosterol, the name given to early preparations of irradiated ergosterol, is essentially synonymous with ergocalciferol.

Ergocalciferol may be used as a vitamin D supplement, and a 2011 clinical guideline considered it to be as effective as cholecalciferol (vitamin D_3) which is produced naturally by the skin when exposed to ultraviolet light.

Toxicity

Toxicity is the degree to which a substance can damage an organism. Toxicity can refer to the effect on a whole organism, such as an animal, bacterium, or plant, as well as the effect on a substructure of the organism, such as a cell (cytotoxicity) or an organ such as the liver (hepatotoxicity). By extension, the word may be metaphorically used to describe toxic effects on larger and more complex groups, such as the family unit or society at large.

1. The _____ is a live (attenuated) virus that protects against the viral disease commonly known as chickenpox caused by Varicella Zoster Virus (VZV). _____ is marketed as Varivax in the U.S. by Merck. Another vaccine that is known as Zostavax and used to reduce the risk of shingles (also called Herpes zoster) and Postherpetic neuralgia is caused by the same virus, Varicella Zoster Virus (VZV), and is simply a larger-than-normal dose of Varivax.

   a. Vi capsular polysaccharide vaccine
   b. Yellow fever vaccine
   c. Varicella vaccine
   d. Synthetic vaccine

2. The _____s, triiodothyronine and its prohormone, thyroxine (T_4), are tyrosine-based hormones produced by the thyroid gland that are primarily responsible for regulation of metabolism. Iodine is necessary for the production of T_3 and T_4. A deficiency of iodine leads to decreased production of T_3 and T_4, enlarges the thyroid tissue and will cause the disease known as simple goitre.

   a. Homeopathic
   b. Thyroid hormone
   c. Leukotriene
   d. Chiropractic

3. . _____ is the chemical name of vitamin D_2, a form of vitamin D.

_____ is a secosteroid formed by a photochemical bond breaking of a steroid, specifically, by the action of ultraviolet light on ergosterol. Viosterol, the name given to early preparations of irradiated ergosterol, is essentially synonymous with _____.

_____ may be used as a vitamin D supplement, and a 2011 clinical guideline considered it to be as effective as cholecalciferol (vitamin D_3) which is produced naturally by the skin when exposed to ultraviolet light.

a. isomer
b. Orphan Drug Act
c. Ergocalciferol
d. Phospho

4. _____, commonly known as shingles and also known as zona, is a viral disease characterized by a painful skin rash with blisters in a limited area on one side of the body (left or right), often in a stripe. The initial infection with varicella zoster virus (VZV) causes the acute, short-lived illness chickenpox which generally occurs in children and young adults. Once an episode of chickenpox has resolved, the virus is not eliminated from the body and can go on to cause _____ often many years after the initial infection.

a. herpes simplex
b. Homeopathic
c. Herpes zoster
d. Pepto-Bismol

5. A _____ is a situation in which a substance affects the activity of a drug, i.e. the effects are increased or decreased, or they produce a new effect that neither produces on its own. Typically, interaction between drugs come to mind (drug-_____). However, interactions may also exist between drugs & foods (drug-food interactions), as well as drugs & herbs (drug-herb interactions).People taking antidepressant drugs such as Monoamine oxidase inhibitors should not take food containing tyramine.Hypertensive crisis may occur(An example of drug-food interactions).

a. JV-1-36
b. Drug interaction
c. Lifestyle drug
d. Low-dose naltrexone

ANSWER KEY
15. UNIT-1S Health Promotion

---

1. c
2. b
3. c
4. c
5. b

You can take the complete Online Interactive Chapter Practice Test

for 15. UNIT-1S Health Promotion
on all key terms, persons, places, and concepts.

No Additional Costs

http://www.Cram101.com

Register, send an email request to Travis.Reese@Cram101.com to get your user Id and password.

Include your customer order number, and ISBN number from your studyguide Retailer.

Want More?
JustTheFacts101.com...

Jtf101.com provides the outlines and highlights of your textbooks, just like this e-StudyGuide, but also gives you the PRACTICE TESTS, and other exclusive study tools for all of your textbooks.

Learn More. *Just click*
http://www.JustTheFacts101.com/

9 781538 835623